Introducing Circle Time to Secondary Students

A Seven Lesson Programme for 11 to 12 Year Olds

Charlie Smith

P·C·P
Paul Chapman
Publishing

Lucky Duck is more than a publishing house and training agency. George Robinson and Barbara Maines founded the company in the 1980s when they worked together as a head and as a psychologist, developing innovative strategies to support challenging students.

They have an international reputation for their work on bullying, self-esteem, emotional literacy and many other subjects of interest to the world of education.

George and Barbara have set up a regular news-spot on the website at http://www.luckyduck.co.uk/newsAndEvents/viewNewsItems and information about their training programmes can be found at www.insetdays.com

More details about Lucky Duck can be found at

http://www.luckyduck.co.uk/

Visit the website for all our latest publications in our specialist topics

- Emotional Literacy
- Bullying
- Circle Time
- Asperger's Syndrome

- Self-esteem
- Positive Behaviour Management
- Anger Management
- Eating Disorders

ISBN: 1 904 315 13 5

Published by Lucky Duck
Paul Chapman Publishing
A SAGE Publications Company
1 Oliver's Yard
55 City Road
London EC1Y 1SP

SAGE Publications, Inc.
2455 Teller Road
Thousand Oaks, California 91320

SAGE Publications India Pvt Ltd
B-42, Panchsheel Enclave
Post Box 4109
New Delhi 110 017

Commissioning Editor: George Robinson
Designer: Helen Weller
Illustrator: Philippa Drakeford

© Charlie Smith 2003

Contents

Chapter 1: Introduction and background   **5**

    What is Circle Time?   6

    The philosophy of Circle Time   6

    The aims of Circle Time   7

    What Circle Time achieves   8

    Skills developed through Circle Time   8

    The link with self-esteem   8

    The link with positive behaviour   10

    The link with spiritual and moral development   11

    The link with PSHE and citizenship   12

    Circle Time and the National Curriculum   13

    The link with speaking and listening   14

Chapter 2: Preparing for Circle Time in your school   **17**

    Circle Time structure   18

    Circle Time application   19

    Working in groups   20

    Setting up Circle Time   22

    The role of the group facilitator   24

    Rules   25

    Encouraging ative listening   27

    Managing emotions   28

    Managing behaviour   29

Chapter 3: Circle Time techniques explained   **35**

Chapter 4: A Circle Time programme   **47**

    Delivering the programme   48

    Session 1: Setting the scene   50

    Session 2: Listening   54

    Session 3: Friends and friendship   62

    Session 4: Respect, consideration and co-operation 73

    Session 5: Anger management   84

    Session 6: Bullying   88

    Session 7: Review, Feedback and evaluation   93

Bibliography   **98**

The Worksheets

To photocopy the worksheets directly from this book, set your photocopier to enlarge by 125% and align the edge of the page to be copied against the leading edge of the the copier glass (usually indicated by an arrow).

Chapter 1

Introduction and Background

What is Circle Time?

Circle Time is a structured, distinctive and creative form of group work, where pupils and the group facilitator sit together in a circle. Group meetings are held regularly, they create a safe, risk taking, trusting and non-blaming environment to speak, listen, share thoughts, explore ideas and interact. Circle Time is a way of supporting young people, raising their confidence and building their self-esteem; it is a tool to encourage them to believe they are worthwhile people. Circle Time creates a caring group feeling where people involved are valued and able to learn more about themselves.

Circle Time is not new to education; pupils from both the primary and secondary sector across the country undertake Circle Time as a regular feature of their timetable. Circle Time is increasingly popular in schools due to the impact of both its content and process in providing a distinctive approach to contributing, influencing and exploring communication skills, and emotional, social and interpersonal development in pupils.

The philosophy of Circle Time

"Circle Time is not therapy. It is not to be seen as treatment of any kind...we are not solving problems in a Circle Time session, but building skills of awareness. Circle Time is an educational model and belongs in a school curriculum along with other content areas. It requires no esoteric leader skills such as are required for counselling or doing therapy or treatment of any kind. No problem, in fact, is assumed. The teacher does not bring to the circle a 'something is wrong and needs fixing' problem mentality, and hence is not interested in analysing, probing or psychoanalysing kids...our experience is that people who simply pick up a book and start leading circles sometimes do so with the mistaken intention of doing some sort of problem solving with students for instance, doing circles to 'reduce discipline problems'....It is designed to be done by teachers or facilitators with no special background other than a caring for children and an appreciation of the role of affective development in a child's experience."

(Ballard, J. 1982 Circlebook)

Current thinking around the concept of Circle Time was formalised by Ballard (1982) who identified ten value statements for its practice. Bliss et al (1995) in adopting Ballard's value statements identified a set of beliefs essential to the process and principles of Circle Time.

- Children are essentially good if they are treated with respect.
- Teachers are in a powerful position, responsible for the environment within which children learn.
- This environment should be supportive and accepting if it is to foster the best development of young people.
- Teachers should be thoughtful about the position of power in relation to pupils, and should avoid using fear to control behaviour. Fear does not enable and it cannot encourage the development of self-motivated young people.
- Teacher's expectations of the ability and worth of a young person are inevitably transmitted and these expectations will affect the self-image of the young person. The teacher, therefore, has a responsibility to convey acceptance and encouragement.
- If young people are to become self-reliant adults, they must be given the opportunity to make choices and to accept the responsibility for the consequences of those choices.
- The ability to make a good decision is dependent on knowledge of self and knowledge of others. In order to achieve this awareness, it is important to be able to identify the needs of self and the needs of the other person and to understand the conflict that may arise in a relationship where these needs are not congruent.
- Understanding of needs and resolution of conflicts depend upon two essential skills; the ability to listen when the other people speak and the ability to speak clearly about ones own feelings.

(Bliss, T., Robinson, G. & Maines B, 1995, P5)

The aims of Circle Time

Circle Time has a host of aims bound in both its process and its content however it can be described that Circle Time aims to develop the individualistic and unique potential of each person and develop and enhance their social, emotional and interpersonal growth. Ballard (1982) describes Circle Time based on achieving the three following functions:

1. Awareness – knowing who I am, the development of self and self-awareness.
2. Mastery – knowing what I can do, the development and enhancement of personal skills.
3. Social interaction – knowing how I function in the world of others, the development and enhancement of social skills.

What Circle Time achieves

Circle Time gives young people the opportunity to:

- understand themselves and express their own individuality
- understand others and increase insight, awareness and sensitivity to others
- appreciate others and the value of friendships
- develop confidence and build self-esteem
- be aware of their feelings and handle them in a healthy way
- resist peer pressure and handle upsets
- enhance social skills such as co-operation, sharing, developing and promoting effective communication
- welcome new challenges and the opportunity to take risks
- promote self-direction and learn from mistakes
- look for alternative solutions and make decisions
- cope with change and difficulty
- develop conflict resolution and problem solving strategies
- enjoy a full life
- have fun, receive affirmation and inject the 'feel-good' factor.

Skills developed through Circle Time

- concentration
- speaking
- assertion
- developing imagination and creativity
- turn-taking
- questioning techniques
- sensitivity and understanding
- friendships
- confidence and self-esteem
- group development
- giving and accepting compliments
- interpersonal development
- affirmation
- co-operation
- listening
- communication
- following instructions
- observation
- extended feelings vocabulary
- problem solving
- conflict resolution
- self-awareness
- mastery
- persistence and motivation
- empathy and compassion
- cognitive skills such as the ability to reflect, predict, question and evaluate.

The link with self-esteem

By self-esteem we refer to the evaluation that the individual makes and customarily maintains with regard to himself; it expresses an attitude of approval or disapproval and indicates the extent to which the individual believes himself to be capable, significant, successful and worthy. In short, self-esteem is personal judgement of worthiness that is expressed in the attitude the individual holds toward himself and the extent to which he accepts or approves of himself. (Coopersmith, 1967)

How much we like ourselves can be an overall judgement or it can relate to specific areas in our lives, i.e. we can have a high opinion of ourselves but dislike certain characteristics. Our self-esteem can be regarded as how we evaluate our self-image, i.e. how much we like the kind of person we think we are. Self-esteem will also be partly determined by how much our self-image differs from our ideal self (the kind of person – part or whole – we would like to be). The greater the gap between our self- image and our ideal self the lower our self-esteem. Low self-esteem could thus be described as disliking, judging or rejecting parts of yourself and high self esteem liking yourself for who you are.

In education, the issue of a child's self-esteem is a vitally important consideration. Self-esteem affects a child's behaviour in all aspects of school life including academic and social. Children with high positive regard are more likely to achieve academically and less likely to be in trouble than children with poor or low self-regard (Bliss, T & Tetley, J. 1993). Children with low self-esteem look for information to confirm their poor view of themselves and behave in a manner, which is consistent with this view. Examples of such behaviour traits include:

- ▸ fear of failure – finds it difficult to try new strategies or will simply refuse to 'have a go', will often destroy work even if it is good or avoid work and use delaying tactics

- ▸ feeling inadequate, useless, incompetent, unpopular and/or of little use – lack in confidence and are unsure of themselves, find it difficult to make decisions, reluctant to join in

- ▸ appearing anxious and/or depressed – reluctant to join in, may become socially isolated

- ▸ rigidity in his/her thinking – negative self-talk about oneself, looks for proof of negatives, sets unrealistic goals for oneself that are either too high or too low

- ▸ feeling uncomfortable with praise – unable to or finds it hard to accept praise, feel unworthy of praise, feels that no one likes them

- ▸ inability to ask for needs to be met

- ▸ being disruptive – personal feelings of frustration and anger, attention seeking

- being critical and jealous of others

- inability to be warm and affectionate – rarely laughs or smiles

- being negative about self, particularly in comparison with others – puts himself/herself down, negative self-talk.

Burt et al (1999) suggest that to value ourselves we need to feel some mastery over ourselves and to experience success. However, to get children with low self-esteem to 'hear' and believe positive messages about themselves can be a challenging task. They say that Circle Time aims to break into these feelings, in a gentle, subtle and safe way it can help young people do this by building up personal and social skills and giving opportunities to experience success and praise and by affirming positive qualities.

Circle Time contributes to self-esteem through

- developing skills and a feeling of competence (e.g. expressing feelings, being assertive, communicating ones beliefs, contributing to decision making)

- praising, accepting and encouraging individuals through their peers and facilitator

- being able to talk positively and celebrate about ones self and achievements

- accepting that things go wrong sometimes and that it should not fundamentally impinge on self worth

- providing opportunities to take risks and have a go

- receiving positive affirmation by peers and the facilitator, and giving compliments to others

- emphasising a sense of equality, belonging, identity, security, trust and support.

The link with positive behaviour

"Circle Time's special strength is the effect it has on behaviour. It's value in training in human relations and interpersonal sensitivity is clear. Children learn to recognise how their emotions and actions are affected by others, and how the emotions and actions of others affect them. They begin to learn new ways of looking at things, they are prepared to experiment with new behaviours and they have the opportunity to reflect on what these experiences mean for them."

(White, M. 1999 p21)

Circle Time has a large influence on behaviour through a range of avenues. Firstly, Circle Time has an impact on self-esteem and as suggested earlier, low self-esteem has an influence over how we think, feel and behave. Therefore, it is sequential that Circle Time has a direct impact on how we conduct ourselves and how we respond to our own feelings. Secondly, the influence of our peer group plays an effective tool for facilitating change in our behaviour, values and attitudes. Circle Time provides an environment in which we can listen to and explore the views of our peers and thus as a result develop, shape or alter our own attitudes and behaviour. Thirdly, the content of Circle Time provides a social, emotional and interpersonal curriculum for young people, thus providing them directly with the opportunity to learn new behaviours and skills required for social and interpersonal interaction. Finally, the process of Circle Time as we shall see later provides a range of teaching methods that promote positive behaviours such as co-operation, turn taking, listening and communicating. In summary, the ways behaviour is addressed via Circle Time are by:

- learning about self and relationships with others
- offering a non-blaming and safe atmosphere that offers a sense of belonging to a group
- peer influence
- acknowledging participants views and feelings ensuring everyone is valued
- the adoption of a facilitative rather than authoritative role where participants are in control
- discussing issues such as bullying, name calling, aggression
- increasing awareness and the development of empathy
- the application of teaching techniques that enhance social skills development.

The Circle Time approach provides a tried and tested framework for the development of whole-school policy on self-esteem and positive behaviour. In 1989, The Elton Report (Discipline in School) was published by government. It made many recommendations to schools regarding whole school behaviour policies. The Circle Time approach can fully meet these recommendations.

The link with spiritual and moral development

The 1996 Education Act (Section 351) sets the National Curriculum within the context of the spiritual, moral, cultural, mental and physical development of pupils. The policy statement addresses these dimensions and seeks to identify opportunities that the school provides for the development of its pupils. The DfES Circular 1/94 similarly states that:

> "The Government is concerned that insufficient attention has been paid to the spiritual, moral and cultural aspects of pupils development and would encourage schools to address how the curriculum and other activities might best contribute to this crucial dimension of education."

Spiritual development is about beliefs and values, the search for meaning and purpose, self-knowledge, relationships, creativity and feeling and emotions (Qualifications and Curriculum Authority, QCA, 1993). Moral development is concerned with human behaviour, especially the distinction between right and wrong and conventionally accepted standards of conduct. It is about ethics and conscience.

Circle Time offers an environment to explore and address these areas of pupil's development. With regards to spiritual development, Circle Time is a time when pupils can explore their feelings, values and attitudes and develop them based on the exploration of their own and others views. Circle Time provides pupils with a safe environment to think about their own lives, share their experiences and listen to those of others as a means of forming opinions. Burt et al (1999) describes the connection between Circle Time and spiritual and moral development as a time where pupils can explore their 'inner life' (i.e. our personal attitudes, values and beliefs). They state that 'after we are able to explore our own inner self it is easier to try and understand the inner lives of others and the development of the skill of empathy'.

In relation to moral development Circle Time again provides an effective forum for development. For example; Circle Time rules are set by the young people themselves and are adhered to in the circle; activities used throughout the Circle Time process involve mutual respect and co-operation; and moral issues such as bullying, aggression, drugs and so forth can be discussed in the circle.

The link with PSHE and citizenship

Personal, social and health education is a fairly recent addition to the curriculum in England. It gained high profile in the 1990s when the chief executive of the National Curriculum Council attempted to make it part of the state school curriculum. The Secretary of State for education has now decreed that citizenship (now under the umbrella of PSHE) should be taught to all children from the ages 3-16 years, also that citizenship is to be a new statutory subject in it's own right in all secondary schools from September 2002.

Citizenship has three main strands:

1. Social and moral responsibility: pupils learn, from the beginning, self-confidence and socially and morally responsible behaviour, both in and beyond the classroom, towards those in authority and each other.

2. Community involvement: pupils learn how to become helpfully involved in the life and concerns of their neighbourhood and communities, including learning through community involvement and service.

3. Political literacy: pupils learn about the institutions, issues, problems and practices of our democracy and how citizens can make themselves effective in public life, locally, regionally and nationally, through skills as well as knowledge. (DfES 2002)

PSHE covers the following areas of education:

▸ Personal education is mainly concerned with the emotional and psychological well-being of the individual. The promotion of self-esteem, regardless of whether this has to be developed by academic, sporting or genuine personal achievement.

▸ Social education is intended to develop collectivism and group thinking. Prepare young people to engage with economic, social and cultural change. It should also equip pupils to make informed judgements.

▸ Health education covers not only eating habits and a healthy lifestyle, but also drug, sex and relationship education.

(Campaign for Real Education 2002)

The scope for Circle Time and PSHE and citizenship links are wide. Not only can direct topics be the focus in Circle Time, for example peer pressure, friendships and relationships, drugs etc., but also many of the areas that PSHE and citizenship education aim to address. These can be further enhanced through the Circle Time process itself. As previously mentioned Circle Time is a way of supporting young people, raising their confidence and building their self-esteem to encourage them to believe that they are worthwhile people. Circle Time aims to develop the individualistic and unique potential of each person and develop and enhance his or her social, emotional and interpersonal growth. The process alone promotes the development of essential social skills from co-operation to communication.

Circle Time and the National Curriculum

Until children begin to feel positive about themselves, until good relationships are established and until there is a calm, safe, caring, well-ordered environment, the national curriculum cannot be delivered effectively to all children (Mosley, 1993).

Research suggests (Curry and Bromfield, 1994; Mosley, 1993) a high correlation between self-esteem and achievement; a child with low self-esteem is less likely to achieve their potential academically or socially than a child with good self-esteem. Thus by enhancing an individual's level of self-esteem one may raise their ability to achieve and, as noted earlier, Circle Time is an avenue for which this can be accomplished.

Establishing good relationships is also possible through Circle Time. Young people are not only taught new skills such as friendship, conflict resolution, being kind and caring, but the process also encourages the appreciation of others. As Bliss et al (1995) state:

> "Circle Time is an inter-related, multi-layered process. Within the circle participants learn about self, learn about others and relate this knowledge to build relationships between individuals and between groups."

If one can create good relationships between pupils within the school environment and an ethos of caring amongst the school members, the foundations for creating a healthy learning environment are established.

Finally, as Mosley (1993) noted, creating a calm, safe, caring and well-ordered environment helps ensure the National Curriculum can be delivered effectively. Again these are aspects that can be promoted and reinforced through Circle Time. Through the establishment of pupil defined rules, co-operative activities, establishing a trusting and risk-taking environment and teaching methods that promote turn taking, self-esteem, listening and respect, a positive learning environment is established which is transferred to the classroom.

The Circle Time techniques can also be applied within the classroom to teach the national curriculum. Using the teaching methods of Circle Time (i.e. sitting in a circle, rounds, free-think sessions etc.) can impact on pupils learning as well as have a positive effect over the social and behavioural environment within the classroom and between class members.

The link with speaking and listening

Jenny Mosley (1993), in her book *Turn Your School Around* describes how Circle Time fulfils the requirements of levels 1-3 for the statements of attainment in English. She notes aspects such as participation as speakers and listeners in group activities, responding to stories and poems, describing real or imagined events, listening attentively, responding appropriately to complex instructions and questioning and commenting.

14

Circle Time is essentially a speaking and listening process. Many of the Circle Time activities, teaching methods and games provide avenues for pupils to speak and listen individually, in pairs, in small groups or as a large group. Through Circle Time pupils learn how to communicate, how to speak confidently and coherently, how to actively listen to other people and how to respond to others verbally and non-verbally.

> "In Circle Time children can take part as speakers and listeners with increased confidence and be actively encouraged to comment constructively. Ideas and information are re-evaluated and logical argument can be practised...Circle Time is about positive communication and interaction."
>
> (White, M. 1999 p20)

Chapter 2

Preparing for Circle Time in your School

Circle Time structure

In all group work there are stages of development. The Chrisyles Model of this talks of group work as having a beginning, middle and end.

The first phase

The first phase is a 'getting to know you' process. This is where procedures are clarified, ground rules are set and standards and expectations discussed. This initial process is very important as it sets out clear guidelines for all to follow and sets precedence for future good practice. Session 1 of any Circle Time programme needs to reflect this. Participants need to be engaged in activities that allow them to familiarise with each other and help them bond as a group. Pupils need to establish their own set of ground rules in the first session. The facilitator also needs to ensure that the pupils understand why they are doing Circle Time and are clear about the aims of the programme. Opportunity must be provided in the first meeting for pupils to voice their expectations. This initial process cannot be removed from a Circle Time programme; it is essential for its functioning.

> "Students can not directly express their own ideas and opinions until they have learned that their peers and the teacher will not reject them."
>
> Schmuck and Schmuck (1987)

The consolidation stage

The middle phase is about communicating with others through listening, verbal and non-verbal skills. Leadership roles and functions become more defined. Through co-operation and decision-making, group members start to develop a trusting relationship and feel more able to talk freely and discuss feelings. As the group becomes more cohesive with time, conflicts become easier to resolve. These skills are learned through working together, learning to negotiate, respecting each other, being empathetic, expressing feelings and being assertive. The middle sessions of a Circle Time programme are specific topics that enhance personal and social skills. The Circle Time techniques or teaching methods are such that they allow for opportunities to communicate, listen, co-operate, decision make and develop relationships with group members.

The final stage

Finally, there is the ending, the tying up of loose ends and the summing up of how things have gone. The final session of any Circle Time programme needs to clarify the learning experiences of each individual. Time needs to be allocated to reflect on the process and content, and the impacts that it has had. This helps pupils sustain the skills that they have learnt or developed and encourage them to use them in a range of life situations. An evaluation of the programme should be undertaken to help refine future practice. The final session, like the first, is an essential part of any Circle Time programme providing a closure for participants and avenue of saying goodbye and well done.

In a similar vein, each lesson plan within the Circle Time programme is structured following the same format. Each lesson starts with an opening activity, is followed by a main activity and finishes with a review, recap and positive end.

Circle Time application

Circle Time can be applied in different ways:

▸ With a whole-school approach the Circle Time programme can be applied via small group work to a given year group. Here everyone in the year group has Circle Time built into their timetable for a set amount of weeks.

▸ With one-off groups the Circle Time programme can be used to raise self-esteem, build friendships and discuss current topics or to aid social development with a small group of children from a given year group.

▸ With class Circle Time the programme can be delivered with whole classes, curriculum groups or tutor groups. The programme can be delivered in its entirety as PSHE or simply help to gel a class and build rapport among pupils and teacher. Sometimes class Circle Time is used as a means of induction to schools to help pupils build new relationships.

▸ When teaching the Curriculum the Circle Time techniques can be used to deliver subject lessons. Here the teaching methods would be applied to deliver the syllabus. For example, the concept of multiplication might be the focus of the mathematics lesson. Sitting in a circle, the maths teacher may start by doing a round of simple multiplications whereby each pupil takes their turn to answer a question. Remember, pupils have the option to pass if they wish. The next stage could involve a math game such as BUZZ. Here a number is chosen, i.e. 3, the pupils, one at a time count from 1 upwards and when a multiplication of 3 is reached the pupil whose turn it is should say BUZZ rather than the number. A further idea may be using a tagline that has a two parts - one being an answer and one being a multiplication question. A pupil is chosen to start and reads their multiplication question. The pupil with the answer has to shout out, the response is then checked and the pupil reads their question out. This is repeated until everyone in the circle has read their question and shouted their answer.

For some subjects i.e. science or English topics from the Circle Time programme can be used directly if the school feels they match the syllabus.

Whatever method is used it is important that all staff in the school are aware of the process and aims of adopting Circle Time.

Working in groups

When people come together a set of 'group dynamics' begins to emerge.

> "Whether or not people take notice of group processes and the affecting factors in group situations, these factors do influence the outcome of group situations and often produce results that either in direction, intensity or nature have not been allowed for in the calculations of the planners. These kinds of consequence are frequently put down to 'human nature'."

Tom Douglas (1983) Group Work Practice

It is important that the Circle Time facilitator is not just an active participant but also an objective observer of the group dynamics. There can be an array of in-group processes at play within a given group. The following highlights aspects to be aware of and can be used as an analytical tool when working with groups of pupils.

Verbal communication

Patterns of communication and differences in the amount of participation of individual pupils may emerge in the group situation. Some pupils may dominate while others may consistently pass. It is the role of the facilitator to observe such patterns and adjust the lesson accordingly to ensure that all pupils participate on an equal and comfortable level.

Non-verbal communication

People's body language, gestures and facial expressions can tell you a lot about the way they feel, their attitude and persona. Picking up on participant's non-verbal language can help the facilitator in a group work situation.

Leadership and influence

The philosophy of Circle Time is that there is no 'formal' leader as such, in that everyone is equal. A facilitator for the group work however is necessary for Circle Time to function and the facilitator will need to be appointed from the start. The facilitator's role is not to exert their influence over the rest of the group but rather to guide the group through the Circle Time process. Pupil leaders may naturally emerge in the group who may or may not exert a strong influence over the rest of the participants. The people who speak most do not necessarily exert the most influence – total silence can sometimes give someone a high degree of influence.

Decision-making procedures

Whether we are aware of it or not, groups are making decisions all the time; some of them consciously and in reference to major tasks in hand; some of them without much awareness and in reference to group procedures or standards of operation. It is important to observe how decisions are made in the group in order to assess the appropriateness of the method of the matter being decided on and to see what effect the method of decision making has on the group members.

Task behaviour

Certain kinds of behaviour are clearly aimed at getting the group task accomplished; we call this task behaviour. Examples for the facilitator to look out for in small and large group work include initiation (asking for or making suggestions as to the best way to proceed), seeking and giving information (the sharing of facts, opinions, ideas etc.), orientation (summarising what the group has done and keeping the group on task) and clarifying (interpretation of new ideas, indicating alternatives and testing for agreement).

Maintenance behaviour

Just as important as task behaviour is the kind of behaviour which helps the group remain in good working order, creating a good climate for task work and good relationships which permit maximum use of member resource. Examples include harmonising (reconciling disagreements and offering compromise), gate keeping (helping others get into the discussion), and encouraging (being friendly, warm and showing acceptance of other contributions through verbal and non-verbal behaviour).

Negative behaviour

In groups we sometimes see examples of negative behaviour, sometimes this can be useful and necessary, but often it is destructive. As a facilitator it is necessary to think about what the reasons may be for any negative behaviour that emerges and how it can be addressed within the group work setting. Some examples of dealing with negative behaviours are provided in the section titled, 'Managing behaviour'.

Membership

For Circle Time to be successful it is important that each of the participants in the group feel that their peers and their teacher accept them. The degree of acceptance or inclusion in the group will determine how they behave, learn and participate in the group. Different patterns of interaction may develop in the group, which gives clues to the degree and kind of membership.

Feelings

Feelings are feelings, they simply happen. How we behave in response to our feelings, however, is a choice with an effect. When people come together and interact feelings are generated. Sometimes these feelings are obvious and are apparent in an individual's verbal or non-verbal behaviour. As a facilitator being able to read the feelings of the individuals in the group can be an important contributor to its success as a whole as well as for individuals. We can repeat exercises we know generate positive feelings and adapt exercises that cause negative feelings for any of the participants.

Norms

Standards or ground rules may develop in a group and control the behaviour of its members. Norms usually express the belief or desires of the majority of the group members – as to what behaviour should or should not take place in the group. These norms may be clear to all members (explicit), known or sensed by only a few (implicit) or operating completely below the level of awareness. Some norms may help the group progress and some may hinder it.

This is not an all inclusive and definitive guide on what to look for when working with groups. It is a difficult task to be an active participant and an objective observer at the same time and it is easier to see the issues involved when watching other groups in operation. The pay-off comes when you are able to influence group dynamics for the benefit of all the individuals ensuring each member is valued and is an equal participant.

Setting up Circle Time

With all things there are always influencing factors at work. With group work there are a number of things that can affect effectiveness, cohesiveness and outcome. These include factors such as whether members are there by choice or not, why people have come to the group, what makes them want to come back every time, what people perceive to achieve from the group, what individual expectations are, whether the groups expectations are the same and whether the group know one another or not. These aspects need to be addressed in Session 1 as explained in the Circle Time structure.

Other influencing factors include how many people are in the group, how long the group is to last, the frequency of meetings, the make-up of the group, i.e. age, gender, religion, class, race etc. and the environment. The checklist below outlines good practice in setting up Circle Time to help ensure the most effective process and successful outcome.

Room

It is important that the facilitator is allocated a room to undertake Circle Time. Using the library or hall creates difficulties and distractions. The room used needs to project a friendly and comfortable environment to create a safe place for Circle Time to be undertaken. Ideally, the same room needs to be used on a weekly basis to provide consistency.

Frequency and duration

The frequency and duration of sessions is governed by varying levels of concentration. The recommended time slot for secondary aged pupils is 45 minutes. This may vary depending on the group size and dynamics of the group. Consistency in sessions is important and it is suggested that they take place on a weekly basis. Sessions stretched over any length of time decrease the chances of pupils retaining the skills.

Seating arrangements

As one would expect from the title, the group work activity takes place in a circle formation. Chairs should be prearranged into a circle ready for the lesson. All barriers need to be removed, desks put to the side of the room and enough space created to allow movement of pupils.

Using the technique of sitting in a circle creates a sense of unity, co-operation and equality; it indicates that everyone in the group, including the teacher, is equal; that there is no 'controller'. Circle seating ensures everyone can be seen and heard; people can make eye contact, which is an important aspect of speaking and listening; the group is working together to support one another; there are no physical barriers such as desks and chairs and everyone is valued as an important member of the group.

It is important to create a relaxed, comfortable atmosphere for the group. It is best to start by letting pupils sit where they like in the circle, rather than being prescriptive and authoritative the facilitator can use games to get the group mixed up and split friendship groups. It is important that the group facilitator sits in the circle with the pupils as an equal. This gives the pupils the message that the facilitator is not a controller but an equal member of the group, which is particularly important in developing an atmosphere of trust between teachers and children. It is also important that the facilitator is an active participant and joins in all the activities.

Numbers

The number of pupils engaged in a Circle Time programme at any one time can vary considerably depending on the application chosen. For small group work the ideal size is about eight. Small groups help personalise individuals in the group and increase their sense of belonging and value to the group. Class Circle Time can be undertaken with larger numbers, the ideal size for larger groups is thirty; numbers that go over this are more difficult to manage. Very large groups can be time consuming; doing a round for example can involve a lot of waiting and very small groups do not provide enough peer support for pupils. Activities for large groups should be short and pupils encouraged to keep answers brief.

Pupils

Putting together a group for small Circle Time is an essential process. Ideally the group should have a varied background of skills, be mixed in gender and be of the same year group. If there are targeted pupils in the group for behavioural needs numbers should be kept to a minimum so that negative and/or disruptive behaviours are challenged and positive role models are prevalent to promote change. In cases such as these the suggestion is two targeted pupils to six role model pupils. Pupils with behavioural difficulties often respond well to the Circle Time environment, they may feel more in control, have more individualised and positive attention and there are vast opportunities to raise self-esteem and help pupils feel good about themselves. Pupils with emotional problems also benefit from Circle Time, the range of techniques applied to deliver the programme ensure shy or withdrawn pupils are included. Circle Time can help develop confidence and a sense of self.

If pupils in the group have learning difficulties there may be a need to differentiate the work for them. This means that worksheets may need to be adapted, learning styles varied and more in-depth explanations given. However, Circle Time is more active and oral than reading and writing, which means that pupils with learning difficulties will perhaps suffer fewer disadvantages in the learning styles than they might in the classroom. Pupils with other special education needs such as visually impaired or hearing impaired pupils can also be included into Circle Time groups as there is support in Circle Time from the teacher as well as peers; the work is of a co-operative, helping and caring nature. Be sure to know the make up of your group to account for their needs and have the appropriate resources.

The role of the group facilitator

The Circle Time facilitator is the key to success of the programme. A teacher, a school based mentor or an external agency, for example an educational social worker can adopt the role of the Circle Time facilitator. The role that the facilitator will play is very diverse; it involves organising sessions, times and venues, preparing work and resources, facilitating sessions and structuring the learning experience and responding to emotional issues. The Circle Time facilitator will be seen as a model for personal and social behaviours as well as attitudes, morals and values. Korfkamp (1997) outlines the 'musts' and 'shoulds' in relation to the role of a group facilitator:

The **musts:**

▸ The group facilitator must make each pupil feel important.

▸ The group facilitator must make each pupil feel valued.

- ▸ The group facilitator must make sure that each pupil is listened to and heard.

- ▸ The group facilitator must encourage participation.

The **shoulds:**

- ▸ The group facilitator should pay attention to what is going on in different groups.

- ▸ The group facilitator should always try to keep pupils on task by every so often clarifying what needs to be done.

- ▸ The group facilitator should always try to encourage positive feedback.

- ▸ The group facilitator should always pay attention to individual pupils when necessary.

- ▸ The group facilitator should always allow pupils to have the same opportunities.

The facilitator needs to participate actively in the process. The input will be most effective when it is seen by the children as a guide, not a judge, pointing out options without labelling them right or wrong, good or bad (White, 1999).

Rules

In all aspects of society we have rules. An analogy I often use with young people is through posing the question, "what would happen on a football pitch if their were no rules?" or, "if we didn't have any laws what might happen?". After this pupils often agree that where people come together to work, to play or to socialise there are a set of rules in use. Sometimes these rules are written down, other times these rules are 'unwritten', that is, we behave or act in certain ways that we believe, based on our culture or value system, are most appropriate for the situation we are in and for the role we are taking.

Circle Time is flexible but, as with all successful structures, there needs to be some consensus of what is acceptable behaviour. Rules are important as they provide a framework within which relationships can develop and grow in a positive way (Curry and Bromfield, 1998).

It is important that the group has ownership over their rules. To do this pupils as a group can free-think and record ideas for Circle Time rules onto a large piece of paper. They can negotiate priorities and select which they wish to use within the group. This way they will own the rules and therefore be much more likely to adhere to them. It also takes the pressure off the leader from being the law-enforcing authority.

Some rules that groups have evolved are:

- listen to one another
- talk one at a time
- respect the ideas and values of others
- keep personal comments positive
- opportunity to pass
- confidentiality.

Once the rules have been decided they can be displayed on the wall for the remainder of the group time together.

To ensure that pupils follow their rules it is important to be clear to the pupils that they are the ones to decide when someone is breaking a rule and what should happen as a result. For example, a pupil could be asked to leave the circle until they feel they can return and follow the rule. Whatever consequence is enforced, be sure that it is a consensus among the group as to whether an individual deserves it; this way the facilitator is not solely responsible for what happens in the group. Individuals making up the group can reflect on one another's behaviour based on the rules that they have decided to operate. This again places ownership on the rules and increases the likelihood of adhering to them. Be sure that pupils, as well as the facilitator, openly acknowledge and praise one another for following the rules.

Two important aspects of Circle Time are confidentiality and passing.

Confidentiality

The contract between pupils should include one of confidentiality. It is the role of the facilitator to ensure that pupils understand the concept of confidentiality and apply it to the group situation. This can be an agreement between pupils that they will not discuss what other pupils have talked about with anybody outside the group. This helps develop a climate of trust setting an ethos where pupils feel able to express themselves and take risks. It is important to explore confidentiality in the early stages of meeting the group with whom you will be working and establish clear boundaries. A verbal contract should be made which all pupils and the facilitator can refer back to. The contract should state what both the pupils and the facilitator is aiming for – what can be expected as well as what cannot be provided.

In conjunction with child protection law, limits to what can be kept confidential will occur if someone discloses they have been physically injured or abused, this includes:

- physical abuse

- emotional abuse

- sexual abuse (includes pregnancy)

- neglect.

Confidentiality of the facilitator may need to be broken if someone is experiencing severe emotional distress, if there are any concerns about the persons safety or welfare, or if the facilitator has any doubts about their ability to assist the pupil.

The pass rule

It is important that pupils who engage in Circle Time do not feel pressurised or uncomfortable participating. The range of Circle Time techniques allow for a variety of ways to engage pupils, so for those that may not wish to speak in front of a large group they have the opportunity to undertake work in pairs, on worksheets or in small groups. It may be that at points in a Circle Time programme a pupil does not wish to participate and in this situation the pupil has the right to pass. At the end of the activity it is important to return to the pupil and allow them the opportunity to answer, contribute or comment if they wish to.

Encouraging active listening

As previously noted, Circle Time is essentially a speaking and listening process. Many of the Circle Time activities, teaching methods and games involve the skill of active listening, a skill that involves offering our full attention to another. Curry and Bromfield (1998) identify ten components of active listening:

1. Having eye contact with the person who is talking.

2. Giving full attention.

3. Sitting quietly without distracting the person who is talking.

4. Focusing on the speakers needs.

5. Showing that you understand.

6. Letting the speaker express feelings without interruption or put-down.

7. Asking no questions.

8. Making no comments of your own.

9. Showing appropriate non-verbal behaviour.

10. Communicating acceptance no matter what the speaker is saying.

It is important that the facilitator also actively listens to group members. Based on what is disclosed, discussed, what values or attitudes emerge and what feelings are expressed it is not the role of the facilitator to give advice, make comments or judgements, provide sympathy or solutions, agree, disagree, argue, praise or blame. The role of the facilitator is to model Circle Time behaviour, they are to simply listen to and accept individuals, to take a neutral role. Active listening is important to provide an atmosphere of co-operation, trust, acceptance and mutual regard.

It is important that the facilitator encourages pupils in the group to actively listen to one another. This can be done through establishing rules, playing listening games, using a talking object and adopting appropriate techniques that encourage listening (see Chapter 3: Circle Time techniques explained).

Managing emotions

Within the group situation pupils may experience a range of both positive and negative emotions (strong feelings). It is important that the facilitator is able to deal with pupil's emotions. As noted earlier, sometimes feelings are obvious and are apparent in an individual's verbal or non-verbal behaviour. As a facilitator, being able to read the feelings of the individuals in the group can be an important contributor to its success as a whole as well as for individuals within it. According to White (1999) the Circle Time facilitator needs to have a 'personal warmth' demonstrated by a good vocabulary of feelings and a sensitivity to emotional needs, the facilitator also needs to be comfortable in dealing with emotional issues.

When we are presented with strong feelings or information that is painful it is natural to feel we need to respond; we do not have to, it is not the role of the facilitator to be a therapist or provide solutions. Listening, understanding and accepting are usually enough. As Bliss et al (1995) state 'the process is intended to help an individual to be aware of her feelings and learn ways to express feelings in a safe environment'.

Follow-ups

It is important that if information is disclosed that either falls within the realms of child protection, if the pupils appears to be experiencing severe emotional distress or if there are any concerns about the persons safety or welfare that the facilitator conducts a follow-up session with the pupil. The follow-up session may be undertaken with the facilitator or the facilitator with a person who is more experienced in handing such situations. If a pupil makes a disclosure within a group situation it is appropriate to acknowledge it by saying something along the lines of, 'that seems like something you can talk to me about when the group has finished, could you stay and talk to me at the end?'

Circle Time helps enhance self-esteem and confidence, thus pupils with emotional problems benefit immensely from engaging in group work of this nature. The facilitator needs to ensure that a positive ethos develops within the group and that there are ample opportunities for affirmation, positive self-review and praise, and that a range of activities are included to promote this.

Managing behaviour

As noted earlier, within group situations negative behaviours may arise. It is important that pupils with behaviour problems are not simply excluded from group work such as Circle Time as much of the time this type of support helps challenge and change behaviour patterns. Increasing the self-esteem of pupils so they feel better about themselves can have huge impacts on behaviour. To help avoid behaviour incidents in the group, and address them if they should arise, the check list below describes a number of strategies and forward planning principles that can be of use to the facilitator.

Gaining quiet

Circle Time involves playing games and games can become very noisy. Groups can also become noisy on their own, for these reasons it is important for the facilitator and the participants to agree a signal that indicates the need for quiet. This can be a clap of the hands, the blow of a whistle or a bang on the wall. Inform the pupils that any time they hear this signal they need to return to their seats and stop talking. If the group finds this difficult make this a fun exercise, i.e. the first person gets a prize and the last person has to play a simple (but fun) forfeit.

Clear rules and expectations

Ensure that a set of group rules has been devised, that they are clear, that pupils understand them and that they are displayed. Try and phrase the rules positively stating the behaviour that you want. For example, rather than the rule 'don't all talk at once' state the rule as 'one person to talk at a time; raise your hand to signal to talk'. Make sure any new rules that are introduced into the group, i.e. rules for a game that is to be played, are given clearly and concisely. Use the rules to praise pupils when they are good, offer negative consequences as a choice. Ensure that when dealing with a negative situation you label the act and not the child (i.e. "I like you but I don't like it when you choose to interrupt other people", rather than,"you are a rude person").

Opportunities for praise

Catch the pupils being good. Even difficult pupils are good sometimes, be sure to praise them if they are doing the right things. Most people watch for negative behaviour. Use at least three times as many praise statements as negative ones. Try to start and finish every Circle Time session with a positive.

Start every session with a clean slate – give everyone a chance to choose positive consequences first.

Forward planning

Don't just turn up for Circle Time at the same time as the pupils; you will need to forward plan. Make sure the room is ready, materials are prepared, their work is displayed on the wall, the rules are up and so forth. Ensure that you know the lesson plan, make sure that the activities in the lesson plan fit the group that you are working with and keep the lesson clear, interesting and moving at a brisk pace.

Use incentives

The uses of games in Circle Time are excellent incentives for pupils. Games can be used as an incentive for finishing an activity. Other incentives may be personalised to the individuals in the group.

Have a sense of humour

By integrating your own sense of humour, sharing yourself with the pupils and being an active part of the group you will help bridge a relationship with the pupils. The impact of this on behaviour is enormous.

Look for causes of problems

Analyse any problems after the session. It is important to ask yourself why the problem occurred and what the source of the problem may be. Sometimes there is a simple solution that can be acted on. It may be that a follow-up session is needed with a pupil or pupils who are causing particular difficulties and they are set an individual target for the group to help them stay focused and on task.

Promote pupil responsibility

Prepare the rules as a group, allow pupils to decide on consequences (positive and negative), allow pupils to choose a game, allow pupils to contribute, give pupils different responsibilities, use peer tutoring, offer choices, etc. Ensure pupils are in control over their participation, i.e. allow them to pass; pupil responsibility is empowering and allows pupils develop their own learning environment.

Facilitator behaviour

Ensure you are a model for the pupils, be confident in your approach; show good non-verbal communication; use positive and clear language; have a positive belief and attitude and build relationships with pupils. The behaviour of the facilitator, the language they use and the choices they make can have a profound impact of the pupils and the success of the group.

Use games

Games are an excellent tool in Circle Time. If you feel that the groups needs a legitimate reason to move, needs a boost of energy, needs to laugh or inappropriate pairings or groups need to be split up simply play a game. Have a bank of games in reserve that you can call on. Games mix pupils, achieve quiet and help refocus; use them to your advantage. Some examples you may use are:

Change Seats

Aims: Mixing, legitimate movement, fun

Resources: None

What to do: Based on a theme (i.e. cars, desserts, fruit, countries, etc) choose four categories (i.e. for cars it could be Mini, Escort, BMW, Ferrari). Going around the circle, label pupils in turn based on your four categories. Explain to pupils that when you call out a category those who have been labelled as that category are to get up and change places. When you call out the phrase (i.e. motorway, dessert tray, fruit basket, globe – an imaginative phase that encapsulates all the categories) they should all get up and change places.

Chinese Fingers

Aims: Concentration, fun

Resources: None

What to do: Sitting in the circle pupils face the back of the person sitting on their left. A pupil is chosen to start and they draw a simple shape or a number on the back of the person they are looking at. This pupil then copies the shape or number they think was drawn onto their back onto the back of the pupil they are facing. This continues around the circle until it reaches the last person in the circle who states the number or shape they believe was drawn on their back.

Copy the Leader

Aims: Concentration

Resources: None

What to do: In the circle a leader is chosen who starts a simple movement. All pupils are to copy the movement. Once all pupils have got the movement the leader adds another movement. This continues until the movements are too complex to remember. A variation on this is that prior to the leader being chosen one or two pupils are sent out of the room. When the leader has been decided they re-enter and their task is to guess which pupil is leading the group.

Balloons

Aims: Legitimate movement, fun

Resources: Balloons

What to do: You will need three to four blown up balloons for a small group and six to eight for a large group. The facilitor explains that the object of the game is to keep the balloons in the air at all times. Each person however must remain in their space in front of their chair, the can reach inwards, outwards or sideways to prevent the balloon from touching the floor.

Touch Down

Aims: Legitimate movement, concentration, balance, fun

Resources: None

What to do: Ask pupils to form pairs. The facilitator calls out a number. The pupil's task is to have the equivalent number of points (feet, elbows, hands, knees) touching the floor. The last person to touch down with the right number of points is out; continue until there is a winner. Pupils can form groups of three, four of five to make the task more difficult.

Number Change

Aims: Legitimate movement, mixing pupils, fun

Resources: none

What to do: Number each pupil in the circle as well as the facilitator. The facilitator removes their chair and stands in the centre of the circle and calls out two numbers. The pupils who are those numbers have to get up and change seats. The facilitor aims to steal one of the vacant chairs to leave one of the pupils without a seat. The pupil standing now shouts out two further numbers again they change seats. Continue until the group is mixed.

Simon Says

Aims: Communication, concentration

Resources: None

What to do: The facilitator gives a range of instructions for pupils to follow, for example 'put your hands on your head, touch your left knee, raise your rights arms, point to the door, touch your nose'. When the instruction is given with the sentence 'Simon says...' in front of it pupils should follow the direction, if it does not start with this then pupils should not follow the instruction. When a pupil follows an instruction that didn't start with 'Simon says' they are out. Continue until you have a winner.

Ignore minor disruptions

Rather than focus on minor disruptions, direct your attention onto a pupil that is displaying the behaviour that you want to achieve in the group and make a clear positive statement. For example if a pupil is fidgeting and you need them to be still turn your attention to a given pupil, use their name and say: "Thank you XXX you are sitting very still, that is what I need for this activity". By doing this you are not giving negative attention to a specific pupil, you are being clear about your expectations and you are catching pupils being good.

Chapter 3

Circle Time Techniques Explained

Games

Games are a core aspect of Circle Time and they serve a number of functions. Games can be used as a warm-up activity at the start of a session or a reuniting activity at the end of a session, they can be used as a tool to entice pupils into wanting to continue the session and programme (particularly in the first session) and they can be used as an incentive to finish activities. Games can be used to enliven the proceedings after a heavy discussion period, to allow legitimate movement or as a method of refocusing the group. Games can be used to promote fun and laughter and bond the group. They can help pupils get into the pattern of working as a group co-operatively and respectfully.

Name games

At the start of a Circle Time course, games can be played to help participants familiarise with each other and remember each other's names. Name games can also be used through the course of the programme to create unique identities and individuality. For example, Charlie can be Cheerful, Happy, Articulate, Realistic, Lively, Intelligent and Energetic.

Mixing games

Games are a good way to help split inappropriate pairings and friendship groups. Naturally when pupils come to the circle they will sit with who they are more familiar with or someone of the same gender. Games can be used to mix pupils and change who they sit next to. By using a game to mix pupils the facilitator is able to increase the range of pupils that an individual will work with throughout the course of the Circle Time programme. Separating peer groups, inappropriate groupings and friendships through games prevents the facilitator been viewed as authoritative or law enforcing.

Theme games

Games can also be used to initiate, promote and extend discussion on topics, such as co-operation, listening and communication. By asking pupils questions such as 'what skills were needed to play the game?', 'how were the skills applied?', 'what could be done better next time to make it work more effectively?' the facilitator can promote a discussion on a specific topic. Following games, further discussions can be created; pupils can give examples of how they can use these skills in other areas of their life. Using games as a method of teaching is fun for pupils and is an effective method to develop social skills.

The games are fun and useful and if used correctly, can develop a variety of skills. Games can:

- diffuse tension
- break down pupil/teacher barriers
- improve group functioning and co-operation
- promote communication
- encourage creativity and lateral thinking
- enhance self-esteem
- enhance questioning techniques
- encourage instruction following.

- initiate group work skills
- build trust
- improve speaking and listening skills
- increase concentration
- stimulate thinking about behaviour
- encourage eye contact
- encourage turn taking

Rounds

A round is simply where the focus of attention is on one person at a time. It involves turn-taking by going around the circle in a clockwise or anti-clockwise direction. A round gives each group member the chance to make a contribution to the focus of discussion. One person starts, sometimes with an opening tag line such as "I feel proud when…", "I am good at…", "The thing I care about most is…", "Today I feel…", and the turn moves around the circle until everyone who wants to has had the opportunity to contribute. There are no right or wrong answers and no-one, not even the facilitator, is to comment or make judgement about what another person says. This helps participants take risks on voicing their opinions and ideas, and feel at ease in expressing their views. It is also non-judgemental so all ideas are equally valued.

Using a round has a number of advantages. It allows everyone, including shy pupils and the facilitator, to contribute equally. It prevents the 'talkers' from domineering the discussion whilst allowing them to have a contribution and it gives the communication in the group a structure.

When using rounds there are a number of important points to remember. Firstly, one person is to speak at a time while everyone else is listening and secondly, there is an opportunity to 'pass'; this is important when discussing personal or sensitive issues. At the end of the round, the facilitator can ask those who passed if they now wish to speak.

Tag line rounds

A tag line round is when the facilitator structures a sentence that the pupils are to complete ('something I did this week was…','I am a good friend because…', 'co-operation means…'). Tag lines can be given verbally or they can be written down on card. Each pupil in the circle can complete the same tag line or can be given a different tag line on the same theme. Another method of using tag lines includes having a stockpile of tag cards that are turned face down and turned by pupils one at a time and completed.

Speaking rounds
A speaking round is simply where each pupil in the circle takes it in turn to make a contribution to the discussion. There are no prompts as such just a focus for discussion and pupils are free to comment openly, but in turn.

The talking object
To encourage the rule of only one person speaking at a time it is sometimes useful to have an object to pass around that indicates whose turn it is to speak. Only when a pupil is holding the object can they talk. The object can be passed around the circle during a round, or left in the centre of the circle for pupils to pick up at any time they want to contribute. As a group, you could decide on a name for the object.

Writing rounds
Pieces of paper or worksheets can also be passed around the circle for pupils to add their contributions to in turn. Or free-think sessions (described below) can be done in rounds.

Round games
Many games can also be played using this technique. Story telling whereby one person speaks and the next adds to the story continuing around the circle. Remembering games such as 'I went to the supermarket and I bought…' are also fun round games that promote specific skills.

If groups are too large, problems can occur with this technique when pupils have to sit for a long period of time without activity other than active listening, i.e. for those at the start or the end of a round. In cases such as these, make rounds one word answers, i.e. 'today I feel…happy, sad, angry, etc.' and elaborate on these after the round either in smaller groups or pairs. Alternatively pupils can work in small groups or pairs to discuss the topic and then feedback in round style.

Curry and Bromfield (1994, 1998) suggest the techniques of 'double circles' for large groups. They suggest creating two circles of pupil's one facing inward and one facing outward, so each pupil has a partner. A subject or tag line is then given for discussion and taking turns each pupil talks and then listens. After a set time the inner circle of pupil are asked to move one space to their right, so everyone is now facing a new partner. The same subject can be discussed or a new one introduced.

Rounds can develop a variety of skills including:

- turn taking

- speaking and listening skills

- enhancing self-esteem

- eye contact

- instruction following

- stimulating thinking about behaviour.

Free-thinking

One effective technique for gathering ideas about a specific issue, word or area or even suggestions for solution is free-thinking. A large piece of paper is placed centrally in the circle and each pupil is provided with a felt-tip pen. The facilitator writes a prompt, word or dilemma in the centre of the sheet of paper and then asks pupils to record their ideas about the prompt. Pupils can simply write on the paper as they form ideas or the facilitator can ask pupils to raise their hand if they have an idea, so that recording the information is done in turns. Alternatively the facilitator can scribe as the pupils voice their ideas, or ideas can simply be aired without being recorded. During free-think sessions pupils are asked to contribute ideas without commenting on anyone else's, all ideas are recorded and acknowledged. The technique should be non-judgemental with everybody's ideas being valued and accepted, comments about ideas should not be made. It is appropriate for the facilitator to add their ideas as an active participant in Circle Time. After pupils have exhausted their suggestions, the list can be reviewed, categorised, simplified, placed in order of importance or discussed in more depth. Free-thinking produces a large number of ideas on a given area quickly; allows participants to think creatively and contribute original ideas; involves everyone and shows that by working together more can be achieved – 'two heads are better than one' as the saying goes.

Tag free-thinking

The facilitator records a tag line for pupils to complete in the centre of the paper, i.e. 'friendship is…being there, caring, supporting, sharing, being honest, company, playing together' etc.

Dilemma and solution free-thinking

The facilitator records a dilemma or problem in the centre of the paper and the pupils are to record a range of solutions, for example, 'when Jamie first started school he didn't know anyone, what could he do?' Possible solutions are: join school clubs, ask for a mentor, introduce himself to people, ask if he can join in, etc. Once all solutions have been recorded they can be discussed in more detail, categorised or rank ordered from most effective to least effective.

Word association and meaning free-thinking

The facilitator records a single word on the piece of paper and asks pupils to think of others words that mean the same, then record short sentences about the word's meaning, i.e. anger - mad, fury, hot, vexed, heart pounding, annoyed, something you feel, hitting, etc.

Picture free-thinking

The facilitator can write a sentence, word or tag on the paper and pupils have to cut out pictures from magazines that they feel represent this word and stick them on the paper. The opposite is that the facilitator puts a picture in the centre of the page and the pupils have to record things about it, for example what they think is happening, how they feel about it, or what the solutions or causes may be.

For very large groups free-thinking sessions can be done in smaller groups each having the same task or each having a different task. The same methods can be applied in these smaller groups and reporting back can look for common themes. Alternatively pieces of paper can be placed around the room at different workstations each with a different free-thinking task related to a common topic. Pupils are split into small groups and rotated around the workstations; they are given a set amount of time at each of the workstations to record their ideas. The group is reconvened and pupils are chosen or volunteer to report back.

Discussions

A discussion is an open forum where a topic is introduced to the group and guided by the facilitator using open questioning to prompt thinking. Pupils are free to make comments and contribute thoughts and opinions. Discussions, like free-thinking, give pupils the opportunity to share and express their views in a non-judgemental climate. It is important that rules such as turn-taking, listening, talking one at a time and respecting ideas and values, are adhered to during discussions. This ensures pupils feel valued and equal with everyone else and have the feeling that their contributions are necessary and will be heard. Discussions are a productive technique, they help pupils develop an awareness of ones self. Through making statements about what they believe in, who they are, how they feel and what they like they are able to learn about themselves as well as other people. Discussions give pupils insight into the world of others, in that some people experience, think, feel or go through the same situations as them whilst others may experience the same incident but have different feelings, behaviour, outcomes and experiences. Discussions help pupils express themselves both verbally and non-verbally. Ballard (1982) indicates four ways in which Circle Time influences self-understanding and awareness, that are relevant to the discussion and many other Circle Time techniques:

1. Focusing on a particular topic or statement and understanding its implications.

2. Hearing other peoples contributions and comparing them with our own perspectives.

3. Learning to disclose openly only what is comfortable to communicate at that time.

4. To receive feedback by watching and listening to the responses of the group and learning from this feedback.

Discussions can take place with the whole group or the pupils can divide up into smaller groups and then report back to the circle. White (1999) stresses that discussions are more successful in small groups than larger ones and for this reason when working with larger groups, particularly whole classes, we should split them up. White talks about the importance of forming groups and that random allocation to grouping should be used rather than friendship. He suggests that this could be done through creative methods such as groups of the same hair colour, same month birthday, same number of letters in their name, etc. White points out that the best psychological number of a group of this nature is 3, a triad and that sometimes it is more effective to bring two triads together for feedback prior to reforming the large group and taking comments.

Discussions can develop a variety of skills including:

▸ encourage turn taking

▸ speaking and listening skills

▸ debate

▸ interpretation

▸ commenting

▸ communication – verbal and non-verbal

▸ enhancing self-esteem

▸ encouraging eye contact

▸ self-awareness

▸ self-understanding

▸ encouraging the understanding of differences and acceptance of difference.

Worksheets

A worksheet in Circle Time allows differentiation in learning style. Circle Time worksheets are usually kept very simple and do not take long to complete. Completion is usually individual but can be done in pairs or threes. Worksheets give pupils the opportunity to express and reflect upon their own opinions, beliefs, inner feelings or thoughts on an area before listening to others in a group. Within a peer group situation, particularly when the group is new, pupils are more likely to give their peer group answer and conform to the group norm when talking openly. By asking pupils to complete a worksheet individually prior to discussion further within the group situation, gives pupils a chance to express their individual response. In a similar vein some pupils in the group situation may not contribute verbally but will do so via written exercises, thus through varying the learning style it is possible to include all pupils actively in the process. Some individuals have not yet formed opinions or beliefs about specific areas and individual work allows them time to reflect on issues personally before listening to group responses. Both methods are important as noted by Ballard (1982) earlier, Circle Time allows pupils to disclose openly what they are comfortable with, develop self-understanding and hear other people contributions and compare them to their own.

Reconvening the group and discussing worksheets is an integral part of the exercise as it allows pupils to verbalise their opinions and listen to the views and opinions of others. When feeding back responses from worksheets it is important to express that there are no right or wrong answers and that if pupils wish to pass they can. Pupils may want to share certain parts of their worksheet or the facilitor may pose a series of open-ended questions to prompt further thought. Respecting one another's views is vital in this exercise so that each pupil feels valued and that their point, belief, feelings and opinion is felt valid even if it is different to others.

Worksheets are also useful as pupils can take them away after the end of sessions and use them as a reminder.

Drama and role-play

Drama is where the group either creates or is given a situation with a sequence of events and a script to act out or perform. Role-play can be an activity in which a person imitates, consciously or unconsciously, a role uncharacteristic of himself or whereby a person remains in character to practise a series of skills and tries to implement them after learning them in theory.

Drama and role-play act as valid learning experiences especially for those who are visual and kinaesthetic learners. It is important, however, to be mindful of those pupils who find this technique difficult and uncomfortable and create other roles for them to play if necessary, i.e. observer or director. Drama and role-plays can be used in a multitude of ways to help children explore ideas, thoughts, feelings, solutions and consequences. They can be used to reinforce skills, practise them in a safe environment and generally allow pupils to have a go at applying new skills.

By giving pupils a character they are stepping into someone else's shoes. However, pupils can only express what they know, their thoughts, their feelings and their behaviour. Through using a character a safe environment is created for pupils to express their views in front of their peer group. Also by introducing new ways in which their character can think, feel or behave we can encourage alternative thinking patterns without an individual feeling they are being challenged directly.

Amongst other skills, drama and role-play enhances pupils' confidence, encourages creativity and imagination, and promotes good communication.

Journals, diaries and think books

Curry and Bromfield (1994) introduce the ideas of using journals and think books in Circle Time. They say that some pupils find it too threatening to actually voice their thoughts and feelings and that by having an alternative method to record them, committing concerns and worries to paper provides an outlet for emotions, thoughts and anxieties that might otherwise be an unreleased burden. They suggest that the teacher can either record tag lines in the book or allow pupils to record thoughts and feelings freely as a diary entry.

Giving all pupils in Circle Time a simple diary to take away is one means of self-monitoring. They can be asked to record specifics such as how they felt each time they became angry or the positive comments that they received during the week. Diaries are particularly useful in Circle Time when you are returning to a particular topic. They can be used as a tool to develop self-awareness and understanding. Pupils can bring their diaries to Circle Time sessions and talk about their entries with the group if they feel comfortable. Curry and Bromfield (1994) suggest that it may be useful for the facilitator to respond to diary entries by writing back or just acknowledging in some way that they understand the problem and that it is okay. For others their thoughts may need to remain their own and this privacy should be respected.

Poetry

Poetry can be used in different ways during Circle Time. Pupils can be asked to form short poems about topics such as bullying, friendship, hurt and so on.

For some pupils expressing themselves through poetry is powerful, particularly for those pupils who are creative thinkers and rhythmical learners. Using poetry readings and asking the group or small groups to discuss content is a further way of using this teaching method, or simply reading a poem to the large group to reinforce something.

Asking pupils to read, listen to or write poems on a certain topic can aid:

- creativity
- expression of feelings
- literacy
- different learning styles
- expression of thoughts.

Stories

Story telling can be used to illustrate an issue under discussion, to prompt a discussion, to help form solutions or to promote speaking skills. The facilitator or pupils can read stories or extracts from books or magazines. Follow-up exercises can discuss character's thoughts, feelings and behaviours; the group can break into smaller groups and different endings to stories can be made up; if the story involves a 'problem' solutions can be free-thought by the group and pupils can adopt characters from the story, discuss issues based on their character and consequences of actions can be examined. Stories help examine behaviours and feelings from different perspectives – individuals are very self-focused and usually see things from their reference point. Through using a story it is possible to examine the full range of people's views, options and feelings in a given situation enabling children to see different points of view. Stories enable the topic to be looked at safely through the eyes of the characters in the stories, using this technique (called 'one-step removed') pupils can safely discuss their ideas through the characters.

Competitions, quizzes and dilemmas

The aim of Circle Time is not to create a competitive and hierarchical climate, however, engaging older children through setting them competitions, quizzes or dilemmas can be fun. Competitions and quizzes should not be between individuals but large teams where individuals can work co-operatively and interactively as a group. Competitions need not just be written – they can be about designing posters or writing poems. Dilemmas can be given to the large group or small groups; here pupils would be presented with a situation that requires them to work co-operatively together to find solutions to a problem.

Competitions and quizzes allow pupils to practise competitiveness and team opposition in an acceptable way. Dilemmas look at ways of problem solving and aid co-operative working. Competitions, quizzes and dilemmas can be related to the focus of the session and they can make learning fun.

Debriefs

Debriefing is about providing more in-depth information after an activity has taken place. For example pupils may engage in a game and initially they will simply see the game as a means of having fun. During a debrief after the game the facilitator can inform pupils about the nature of the game, the skills that pupils needed to apply to make it work and go on to create further discussions. Debriefs are an important aspect of many Circle Time techniques. The debrief is the way in which children learn and put the theoretical and practical together. Debriefs help pupils understand working practice, available choices and consequences. Debriefs allow time to examine individual perspectives and enable the formation of opinions.

Displays

During the course of the programme a number of posters will be created from the rules of free-thinking and small group work. Try to display these during the course of the programme. Displaying work reminds pupils of the issues they have addressed, demonstrates value for the work that has been completed and increases comfort, safety and co-operation as the pupils are surrounded by positive words and messages.

Folders

One optional suggestion is providing each pupil with a folder to keep copies of the work they complete during the course of the sessions as well as their Certificate of Completion. This encourages pupils to take away the skills they have learnt and enables them to look back at what they have learned and how they have developed.

Certificates

Certificates provide a celebratory end to Circle Time; they affirm pupils' positive achievements throughout the course of the programme. Certificates can be personalised to highlight an individual's positive and/or special qualities demonstrated during the sessions. They can be presented by the facilitator, the head teacher or even in an assembly.

Certificates do not necessarily need to be limited to the end of Circle Time sessions; they can be given during the course of the programme for a whole range of things. Some ideas include best listener sticker, kind person award, good work token, most helpful certificate, etc. It is a good idea to tell pupils how they can gain extra certificates and hand them out at the end of a session; the decision about who should receive a certificate should come from the group and not the facilitator.

Evaluations

It is important that at the end of a Circle Time programme an evaluation is undertaken. This can take the form of a round when everyone is asked to say what he or she enjoyed or did not enjoy about a particular activity, session or programme in general. It can take the form of a written evaluation sheet, picture association, face drawing or other creative methods. Evaluations give the facilitator instant feedback on the pupils' views of Circle Time and can be used to develop future sessions. They also provide an opportunity for the pupils to reflect on what they have learnt during the course of the programme and how they may have applied it to issues in their life. Furthermore, evaluations and reflection sessions enable clarification on areas that individuals may wish to expand, for this reason the evaluation needs to be a session in itself.

Chapter 4

A Circle Time Programme

Delivering the programme

Introducing Circle Time into Secondary Schools comprises of seven group work sessions. Each session lasts roughly forty-five minutes and can be delivered to small groups or class groups. Where necessary adaptations to activities for varying group sizes are provided. Additional sessions to evolve the programme, or extra activities to extend the sessions, can be delivered if the school wishes to add to the package provided. Good practice on preparing to deliver the programme is outlined in Chapter 2 and should be read by the facilitor prior to delivery.

The manual takes the facilitator step-by-step clearly through each session. The aims of each session are stated, lesson plans are provided and all the resources that are required are included in the copiable pages at the end of each session. The sessions are highly interactive and are based on visual, auditory and kinaesthetic (VAK) learning and apply the range of Circle Time techniques discussed in Chapter 3.

Session 1: Setting the scene

This session introduces the concept of Circle Time to pupils and outlines the content of the course. The purpose of this initial session is to create a safe, trusting and positive working environment. Much of the session is allocated to activities that allow pupils to get to know one another. Group rules are established and expectations are discussed.

Session 2: Listening

This session provides opportunities for pupils to identify the skills required for successful listening and to practise listening skills. The session aims to raise pupils confidence in listening, communicating and interacting with others and apply what they have learnt to everyday life.

Session 3: Friends and friendship

Session 3 looks at what friendship is, the difference between friends and acquaintances and the qualities that foster good friendship. The session provides pupils with the skills to make new friends and maintain their current friendships effectively.

Session 4: Respect, consideration and co-operation

Session 4 takes pupils through the terms respect, consideration and co-operation providing them with opportunities to identify the skills required in these concepts. The opposite of these terms are examined and how people feel when they are treated this way.

Session 5: Anger management

Pupils start to examine the triggers to their anger, how they react when they become angry and the consequences that negative anger release can have on oneself and others. Pupils are taken through a range of strategies that can help them to manage anger effectively.

Session 6: Bullying

The concept of bullying is defined and some myths and facts are discussed. There is opportunity for pupils to discuss their personal experiences of bullying. The reasons for bullying and is effects are examined and ways to prevent bulling in school are presented.

Session 7: Review, feedback and evaluation

This final session looks at the skills pupils have developed and learnt as a result of the Circle Time programme. It also aims to clarify any unanswered or unclear areas. Pupils receive a certificate of completion and fill out an evaluation form.

Session 1: Setting the Scene

Aims

- to introduce the concept and purpose of Circle Time
- to outline the course content
- to build a trusting, safe and positive working environment
- to allow time for pupils to get to know one another
- to establish group ground rules.

Resources

- Dumbstruck Sports Cards
- marker pens
- blue tack
- flip chart.

Introduction

Introduce the concept, purpose and aims of Circle Time and small group work. Highlight the types of activities pupils will be engaging in over the course of the programme.

Name games

My Name
One pupil at a time going clockwise around the circle stands up and states their full name.

Name Chains
One person stands in the centre of the circle, the facilitator calls the name of a pupil and the pupil in the centre has to tap the named person on the head before the named person calls out someone else's name. If the person in the centre is unable to tap the named person on the head before they call out a second name, they must try and tap the second named person on the head; this continues until the person in the centre taps the person on the head whose name has been called, before that person calls another name. A swap of person is made by tapping a person before another named person is called.

Initial Game
One person introduces him or herself and then says something they like or enjoy, beginning with the same letter of their name, for example, "I'm Charlie and I like chocolate." The next person continues, "That's Charlie and she likes chocolate. I'm Thomas and I like tigers." Continue until everyone has had a turn, with the whole group co-operating to help those at the end.

Rules

Every group needs rules in order for it to function properly. There are rules everywhere that we need to stick to, such as school rules and sports rules. Ask the pupils what they think the ground rules for this group should be. Suggestions are:

- speak one at a time
- talk politely and kindly to one another (no put downs, 'dissing' people or their families)
- listen carefully
- respect others' views, opinions and property
- everyone is allowed to have a say
- free choice to pass
- confidentiality
- have fun.

Record rules on to a large sheet of paper and place them on display during this and all consecutive sessions.

Mixing game

Change places if...

- you like pizza
- you have a pet
- you like the cold weather
- you have blue eyes
- your birthday is in June, July or August etc.

Continue until the group is thoroughly mixed and friendship groups are separated.

Getting to know you

Place pupils into pairs (A and B). 'A' becomes the interviewer and questions 'B' to find out as much about her/him as possible. 'A' then reports back to the circle about 'B'. The process is then reversed.

Dumbstruck Sports

Each pupil is given a card on which there is a sport written, there are two of each sport. The aim is for each pupil to find the other person with the same sport as him or her. The difficulty is that pupils must do this without speaking or showing their card to others. They can only mime. If two people believe they have the same sport, they show each other their cards. The game continues until everyone has formed a pair. For larger groups pupils are to work in pairs or threes and act out their sport together until they find their other pair or trio.

Sentence completion

Going around the circle, invite each pupil in turn to complete the following sentences:

- ▸ "I'm happiest when…"
- ▸ "I wish for…"
- ▸ "The most important thing to me in the world is…"
- ▸ "The best thing about being me is…"

Articulating needs

Encourage each pupil to state one or two things that they would like to gain from the group.

Conclude session

End the session on a positive note. Thank pupils for their teamwork, co-operation, kindness etc.

Dumbstruck Sports Cards

TENNIS	TENNIS
SKIING	SKIING
BADMINTON	BADMINTON
CRICKET	CRICKET
FOOTBALL	FOOTBALL
SWIMMING	SWIMMING
BASEBALL	BASEBALL
NETBALL	NETBALL
ROWING	ROWING
DARTS	DARTS
SNOOKER	SNOOKER
RUNNING	RUNNING
GOLF	GOLF
RUGBY	RUGBY
JAVELIN	JAVELIN

Session 2: Listening

Aims

- to provide opportunities for pupils to identify the skills required for successful listening
- to allow opportunities for pupils to practise listening skills
- to highlight blocks to successful listening
- to raise confidence in listening, communicating and interacting with others
- to encourage pupils to apply what they learn to everyday life.

Resources

- Word Halves
- Listening Instruction Cards – one pack between two
- Listening Observation Sheet – one per person
- pens and pencils
- set of keys.

Welcome back and positive start

Welcome back pupils. Going around the circle each pupil is to complete the following round:

"Something I have done well this week is…"

Introduction

Introduce the theme 'listening', highlighting the aims of the session to the group.

Pairing game

Place the word halves into a container and ask pupils to pick out a card. Ensure that you have the exact number of word halves for the number of pupils in the group and no one word half is included without its counterpart. Pupils are to wonder around the room and find the pupil with another half a word that when put together with theirs makes a full word. Once pupils have formed a pair they are to sit back in the circle together. When all pupils have returned read the words in turn.

Are you listening to me?

Based on the pairs formed in exercise three, form 'A' and 'B'. Pupils are to find a space in the room and sit opposite one another. Provide pairs with the stockpile of instruction cards; they should be placed between them face down.

'A' is to take an instruction card from the stockpile, which is to remain unknown to 'B'. 'B' begins a conversation. Ideas for topics could include:

- what I have done since I got up this morning
- what I like about school
- hobbies and interests
- my family
- what I did at the weekend
- what I would change about schooling.

'A' responds to 'B's conversation according to his or her instruction card. Allow one to two minutes for the conversation and then reverse roles using a new instruction card. Continue until all instruction cards have been used.

Debrief

Reconvene the group and discuss the following prompts:

- How did it feel when you weren't listened to?
- How did it feel when you were listened to?
- How did it feel when you weren't listening?
- How did it feel when you were listening?
- What helped you to listen well? For example, eye contact, relaxed posture, concentrating, leaning forward etc.
- What hindered you from listening? For example, not concentrating, not maintaining eye contact, thinking of something else, fiddling with something etc.
- What other things may affect your ability to listen well, particularly in lessons? For example, noise, temperature, boredom, not understanding the subject, feeling emotional, tiredness, feeling unwell, people talking etc.
- Why is it an advantage to be able to listen well?

Clarify the skills required for good listening or in demonstrating to a third party that you are listening:

- relaxed posture
- maintaining eye contact
- clarifying what has been said by questioning or repeating the main gist
- maintaining concentration
- leaning forward
- nodding of the head
- 'umm's' and 'ah-ha's'
- showing interest
- being understanding of the other person
- asking questions if you don't understand.

Practising my listening skills

Form groups of three or four and decide who is 'A', 'B' and 'C'. The role of 'C' could be shared between two pupils if necessary.

'A' is the speaker.

'B' is the listener.

'C' is the observer.

Provide 'C's with an observer's sheet and explain that they are to watch 'B' as they listen to 'A' and to observe and record which behaviours they display as a listener. Explain that some behaviours are verbal (that which is spoken) and that others are non-verbal (that which is unspoken) and are in the form of body language, movements and expressions.

'A' begins a conversation. Ideas for topics could include:

- what I have done since I got up this morning
- what I like about school
- hobbies and interests
- my family
- what I did at the weekend
- what I would do if I won a million pounds.

'B' is to join in the conversation and demonstrate good listening skills.

'C' is to observe 'B' and complete the observation sheet.

After two to three minutes allow feedback on what was observed. Comments should start with what 'B' did well as a listener followed by any comments about where improvements may be required.

Allow time for each pupil to take the role of listener, speaker and observer.

Reconvene group and discuss the activity, allowing pupils to make comments on their listening skills and their non-verbal behaviours.

Recap

Explain briefly to pupils that they have learnt about an extremely important skill in communicating with others. Communication is not simply talking, it also requires listening carefully and asking questions. Communication is a two-way process that requires both parties to be actively involved. Listening involves many skills; briefly recap on these and the blocks that may hinder listening.

Helps Listening

- ▸ relaxed posture
- ▸ maintaining eye contact
- ▸ clarifying what has been said by questioning or repeating the main gist
- ▸ maintaining concentration
- ▸ leaning forward
- ▸ nodding of the head
- ▸ 'umm's' and 'ah-ha's'
- ▸ showing interest
- ▸ being understanding of the other person
- ▸ asking questions if you don't understand
- ▸ feeling comfortable in your surroundings.

Hinders Listening

- ▸ not concentrating
- ▸ not maintaining eye contact
- ▸ thinking of something else
- ▸ thinking of what you are going to say next
- ▸ fiddling with something
- ▸ noise
- ▸ temperature
- ▸ boredom
- ▸ not understanding the subject
- ▸ feeling emotional
- ▸ tiredness
- ▸ feeling unwell
- ▸ feeling hungry
- ▸ feeling uncomfortable and switching off
- ▸ feeling self-conscious
- ▸ day dreaming.

Ending activity

Magic Keys
Place a chair in the centre of the circle with a bunch of keys underneath. Choose a pupil to sit on the chair and blindfold them. Choose another pupil (unknown to the pupil in the centre) to try and steal the keys. The pupil in the centre has to guess, by pointing, where the pupil stealing the keys is coming from. Swap roles.

Story time
Each pupil in the circle is given a number. Choose a pupil to start telling a story, at any point the pupil can stop and call out a number. The pupil whose

number is called has to continue telling the story. Characters in the story must remain the same and the story has to flow.

Conclude session

End the session on a positive note. Thank pupils for their participation, co-operation, enthusiasm, willingness to learn etc.

Word Halves

LADY	BIRD
DUST	BIN
TELE	VISION
ARM	CHAIR
HAND	BAG
SAFETY	NET
BOOK	SHELF
EGG	SHELL
FOR	TUNE
CO	PILOT
SEAT	BELT
HIGH	LIGHTER
IS	SUE
LIVER	POOL
MIN	US

Listening Instruction Cards

Take part in the conversation but do not look the speaker in the eyes	Take part in the conversation and smile and be interested	Listen quietly to the speaker and say nothing	Take part in the conversation but lean far back
Take part in the conversation but stare at the speaker	Take part in the conversation asking related questions	Deliberately think of something else while you are listening	Take part in the conversation and lean slightly forward towards the speaker
Take part in the conversation but fidget with your clothes	Take part in the conversation and nod your head to encourage the speaker	Take part in the conversation but keep looking at your watch	Take part in the conversation and mirror the speakers body language
Take part in the conversation but stand stiffly to attention	Take part in the conversation but turn side ways to the speaker	Take part in the conversation but yawn a lot	Take part in the conversation maintaining good eye contact
Take part in the conversation but keep scratching your nose	Take part in the conversation but keep a blank expression on your face	Take part in the conversation but act more interested in something else	Take part in the conversation and show you are interested and relaxed

Listening Observation

NAME _____   OBSERVED BY _____

Tick the behaviours that you observe in the listener

Posture	☐ leans forward ☐ leans back
	☐ slouches ☐ upright
	☐ relaxed ☐ tense
Voice	☐ loud ☐ quiet
	☐ fast ☐ slow
	☐ boring ☐ interesting
	☐ mumbled ☐ clear
Eye contact	☐ a lot ☐ some ☐ none
	☐ staring
	☐ looking and looking away comfortably
Distance	☐ close ☐ far away ☐ just right
	☐ partner appeared comfortable
	☐ partner appeared uncomfortable
Um's and Ah-ha's	☐ a lot ☐ some ☐ none
	☐ appropriate places
	☐ inappropriate places
Facial Expression	☐ relaxed ☐ tense
	☐ smile ☐ frown ☐ blank
	☐ changes with speakers expression
Movements	☐ nodding head ☐ no head movement
	☐ a lot of body movement
	☐ some movement
	☐ no movement
	☐ fiddling/scratching/leg swinging/shifting position
Questions	☐ a lot ☐ some ☐ none
	☐ related to subject
	☐ not related to subject

Session 3: Friends and Friendship

Aims

- ▸ to help pupils to understand what friendship is
- ▸ to highlight the qualities which foster good friendship
- ▸ to distinguish between friends and acquaintances
- ▸ to raise confidence in making new friends and maintaining friendships
- ▸ to highlight that those people we don't get along with are not due to the person but rather the behaviours they display
- ▸ to encourage pupils to apply what they learn to everyday life.

Resources

- ▸ flip chart prepared with friendship tag line
- ▸ blue tack
- ▸ marker pens
- ▸ Friendship Game Cards
- ▸ Prompt Cards.

Welcome back and positive start

Welcome back pupils. Going around the circle each pupil is to complete the following round:

"Something I have achieved this week is..."

Introduction

Introduce the theme of friends and friendship, highlighting the aims of the session to the group.

A friend is...

In the middle of the circle, place a piece of flip chart paper. Beforehand draw on it a picture of a person and write the unfinished sentence – "A friend is..." For example:

A FRIEND IS...

Ask for volunteers to write a word or a short sentence relating to what they believe a friend is. For example, someone who you:

- ▶ are close to
- ▶ share secrets with
- ▶ trust
- ▶ spend time with
- ▶ respect.

Pupils can write their own sentence on the paper or ask the teacher to write it for them.

Open discussion

What is the difference between a friend and an acquaintance?

How do friendships develop? For example:

- ▶ communication
- ▶ trust
- ▶ enjoy each other's company.

Friendships don't just happen; they have to be worked at.

What do we need to make friendship work or progress? For example:

- ▶ go out of our way (at times)
- ▶ support and listen
- ▶ be truthful and honest
- ▶ be adaptable.

Going around the circle invite pupils in turn to complete the following round:

"I'm a good friend because..."

Changing rooms game

Change places if:

- ▶ your friends are important to you
- ▶ you believe you are a good friend
- ▶ you have never fallen out with your best friend
- ▶ you often fall out with your friends
- ▶ you have lots of friends
- ▶ you have a few close friends
- ▶ you respect your friends
- ▶ you have friends in other schools.

Alternative: Ask each pupil to state a 'change places if....' sentence relating to friends and friendship.

Polite and positive pointers

Going one way around the circle and then the other, get pupils to complete the following sentence about the pupil next to them.

"This is my friend/acquaintance…I like him/her because…"

Friendship game (Adapted from McConnon, S. 1989)

Object
To end up with a set of cards that describe qualities, attitudes or characteristics that make a good friend.

- ▸ Shuffle and deal three/five cards to each person. Put remaining cards face down in a pile, called the playing pile.

- ▸ Choose someone to start. They may return an unwanted card (creating a second pile, called the reject pile) and take a replacement from the top of the playing pile.

- ▸ Play until the playing pile is exhausted.

- ▸ Players may pass once they have a set of five cards that they wish to keep.

- ▸ Blank cards may be used for a quality of the player's choice.

- ▸ When the playing pile is exhausted players lay their cards face up in rank order, with the card the player feels is the most important on the top.

- ▸ Pupils take it in turns to read what is written on their cards, giving reasons for their choice of top card.

- ▸ If players have difficulty deciding to keep a card, read it in conjunction with the Prompt Card – 'People want to be my friend because….'

For groups larger than ten split the class in to smaller groups providing each with the resources needed for the game. When pupils have exhausted the playing pile and have their five cards reconvene the large group. At this point ask the pupils to rank order their cards from most important to least important. Going anti-clockwise around the circle ask pupils firstly to state which was their most important card and why and then which was their least important card and why.

Things we don't like about others

Every pupil is to think of a behaviour that they don't like. Going around the circle in turn each pupil is to finish the following sentence:

"I don't get on with people who are…"

Examples might be:

> ▸ aggressive
> ▸ rude
> ▸ obnoxious
> ▸ unkind.

Pupils must not name others, only a type of behaviour a person may display.

Point out to the pupils that if we don't like someone, it is generally not the person we don't like but their behaviour. Thus, we should not attack someone as a person but rather the behaviour that you don't agree with. For example,

> "I like you but I don't like it when…(name the behaviour)".

Now, get pupils in turn to re-state the type of person they don't like within a sentence where they are challenging the behaviour rather than the person.

> "I like you but I don't like it when…"

Examples might be:

> ▸ people are aggressive to me
> ▸ I am shouted at
> ▸ I feel afraid
> ▸ I feel treated differently to others.

Conclude session

End the session on a positive note. Thank pupils for their friendliness, kindness, honesty, behaviour, etc.

Friendship Game Cards

My hair is soft	I'm good at PE	I'm popular
I'm talkative	I'm outgoing	I have a computer
I play and tell jokes	I have a lot of money	I don't smoke
I have a boy/girl friend	I laugh a lot	I am good at maths
I am bossy		

Friendship Game Cards

I sulk	I take but don't give	I like to be a leader
I tell people what to do	I make the rules	I dominate others
I say what goes	I can get what I want	I get my own way
I am rude	I can manipulate people	I tease
I call people names		

Friendship Game Cards

I argue a lot	I'm moody	I'm a bully
I'm narrow minded	I'm often angry	I think I am the best
I'm selfish	I'm always right	I don't make fun of people
I'm caring	I put others first	I'm approachable
I'm interested in others		

Friendship Game Cards

I am open to opinions	I am open to suggestion	I'm not judgemental
I'm patient	I'm thoughtful	I'm loyal
I'm honest	I'm respectful	I'm open
I'm kind	I'm understanding	I make time for others
I'm a good listener		

Friendship Game Cards

I can keep a secret	I have a sense of humour	I'm helpful
I'm trustworthy	I gently criticise	I think of other feelings
I share	I'm supportive	I work through arguments
I give as well as take	I like to have fun	I join in with others
I am polite		

Friendship Game Cards

I am up to date with fashion	I go out a lot	I do my homework
I have brown eyes	I'm shy	I don't watch TV
I'm cheerful	I care what I look like	I have lots of interests
My dad owns the local shop	I smoke	I wear glasses
I can run fast		

People want to be my friend because…

People want to be my friend because…

Session 4: Respect, Consideration and Co-operation

Aims

▸ to distinguish between the terms respect, consideration and co-operation

▸ to provide opportunities for pupils to identify the skills required in co-operating and being respectful and considerate

▸ to allow opportunities for pupils to practise skills

▸ to highlight the importance of respect, consideration and co-operation

▸ to examine the consequences and feelings involved when we act disrespectfully, inconsiderately and uncooperatively

▸ to encourage pupils to apply what they learn to everyday life.

Resources

▸ flip chart paper
▸ marker pens
▸ blue tack
▸ prepared jigsaw puzzles
▸ Sentence Completion Cards.

Welcome Back and Positive Start

Welcome back pupils. Going around the circle each pupil is to complete the following round:

"Something nice that was said to me this week was…"

Introduction

Introduce the theme of friends and friendship, highlighting that the aim of the session is to encourage pupils to think about how they may feel if they are left out, put down or not considered. The session also focuses on the value of co-operation and mutual respect for one another.

Defining terminology

Place three pieces of flip chart paper on different sides of the room. One should be headed 'respect', another 'consideration' and the third 'co-operation'. Leave at least four marker pens by each piece of paper. Pupils are to walk around the room and write words or short sentences on each piece of paper representing what they believe the word to mean.

An alternative for a large group is to split the group into three and have three workstations respect, consideration and co-operation. Each group is given a set of coloured markers; one group red pens, another green and the third blue. Groups start by free-thinking words and short sentences about their theme. After three minutes the facilitator calls 'change'. The group take their set of coloured pens with them and move to the next workstation, where they now free-think about the second theme. Continue until all groups have rotated around the three themes. At the end ask pupils to feedback from their worksheet at their station.

Once pupils have finished, return to the circle and discuss the differences between the three words.

Look at and discuss the opposites of these words:

- disrespect
- inconsiderate
- unco-operative.

Dictionary definitions

Considerate(ation)

- thoughtful towards other people
- kind to others
- carefully thought out
- bear in mind
- a fact or circumstance to be taken into account when making a judgement or decision
- resulting from deliberation.

Respect(ful)

- an attitude of admiration or esteem / regard
- the state of being honoured or esteemed
- polite or kind regard or consideration
- respect for people's feelings
- an expression of regard
- to have an attitude of esteem towards
- show or have respect for
- to pay proper consideration for
- treat courteously or kindly
- respectful in showing or giving respect.

Co-operate(ation)

- to work or act together
- joint operation or action
- to be of assistance or willing to assist
- helpful
- acting in conjunction with others.

Co-operation Game 1: Tangled

Two pupils are to leave the room. The remaining pupils link hands in a line. The pupil at the end of the line (one end only) should climb under and/or over the linked arms, and the chain of pupils follows. Once the pupil at one end has weaved their way under and over to the end of the line, s/he must link hands with the person at the other end. The two pupils are called back in, their task to 'disentangle' the group of pupils. Everyone must co-operate together in order for it to work.

Game debrief:

- ▸ Why was the game relevant to the theme of the session?
- ▸ How did you help each other?
- ▸ Did everyone help?
- ▸ Was anyone deliberately awkward?
- ▸ Who was the most helpful?
- ▸ How did you solve the problem?

Now pupils are aware of the skills involved, see if they can play Co-operation Game 2.

Co-operation Game 2: Jigsaws

Preparation

At the end of the session notes there are five sets of elephant pictures. Pupils will work in groups of five for this activity so photocopy enough sets for one per group. Each set needs to be cut up and the parts marked with the letter 'A' put into an envelope marked 'A', the parts marked 'B' put into an envelope marked 'B' and so on for letters 'C', 'D' and 'E'.

Divide the group into groups of five and ask them to sit together in a circle. Provide each group with a set of pictures (, i.e. five envelopes, one marked 'A', one 'B', one 'C', one 'D' and one 'E'). Each member of the group is to have an envelope. Spare pupils can act as observers. Tell the pupils that envelopes are not to be opened until you give the signal.

Give the following instructions:

Everyone has an envelope containing pieces of a jigsaw, but your jigsaw pieces do not fit together to make a picture. Other people have pieces of your jigsaw and you have pieces of other people's jigsaw. The task of the group is to make five identical jigsaw pictures, one in front of each of you. The task will not be complete until everyone has a whole picture in front of him or her.

When you open your envelope and lay your jigsaw pieces out you are not allowed to just take the pieces off other people nor are you allowed to ask for the pieces you want. Pose the question, "How are you going to complete your puzzle?" After discussion, hopefully someone will come up with the solution – you are only allowed to give pieces to other people and each piece must be given to a specific person.

To make the task even harder no one is allowed to speak and non-verbal communication such as pointing, staring, nodding or nudging, is forbidden. When everyone has understood the instructions, give the signal to start.

Game debrief

> ▸ How well did you complete the activity and why?
> ▸ How did you feel during the activity?
> ▸ What did you find hard? What did you find easy?
> ▸ Did you cheat?
> ▸ Why was the game relevant to the theme of the session?
> ▸ Did you find the other members of the group co-operated with one another?
> ▸ What skills of co-operation, communication and consideration were you using?

Sentence completion

Place the set of sentence completion cards face down in the centre of the circle:

> ▸ "Co-operation is needed because…"
> ▸ "Being disrespectful is…"
> ▸ "One way I co-operate with teachers is…"
> ▸ "One way I co-operate with friends is…"
> ▸ "One way I co-operate with family is…"
> ▸ "When I need help, I wish others would…"
> ▸ "I could help others by…"
> ▸ "Working in a group is good because…"
> ▸ "Inconsideration of others is…"

Choose a person to start and ask them to pick up a card and read it aloud. They are to finish the sentence.

For small groups sentence cards can be passed around the circle so every pupil completes each sentence completion card. An alternative to reduce time is to hand out each person in the group a card and ask each to finish the sentence that they have been given.

For large groups the first card can be read and passed anti-clockwise to the next three pupils in the circle. When the fourth pupil is reached, a new sentence completion is taken from the stockpile and again completed by the next three pupils. Continue around the circle until all the sentence completion cards have been completed.

Consequences of actions

Get each pupil to think about a time when they were:

- ▸ unco-operative
- ▸ disrespectful
- ▸ inconsiderate.

As a general discussion, ask the group the following prompt questions:

- ▸ "How do you think the person on the receiving end felt?"
- ▸ "What may be the consequences of your words/motions/actions?"
- ▸ "How did you feel?"

Now ask the pupils to think of a time when they were:

- ▸ co-operative
- ▸ respectful
- ▸ considerate.

Again, as a general discussion, ask the group the following prompt questions:

- ▸ "How do you think the person on the receiving end felt?"
- ▸ "What may be the consequences of your words/motions/actions?"
- ▸ "How did you feel?"

Sentence completion

Going around the circle invite each pupil in turn to complete the following sentence:

"I respect... because..."

For example:

Mother Theresa (curing the sick)

Lenny Henry (Comic Relief)
Teachers
Parents
Older people

Conclude session

End the session on a positive note. Thank pupils for their co-operation, consideration for others, respectfulness, etc.

A

B

C

C

C

79

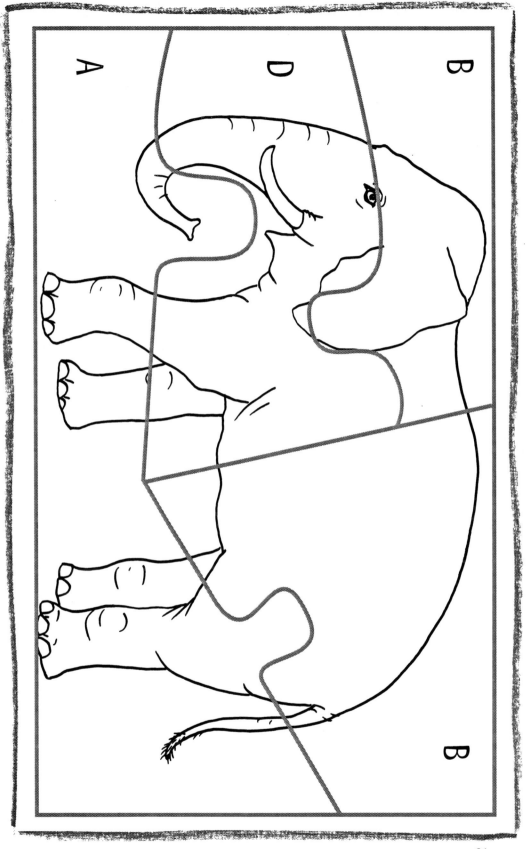

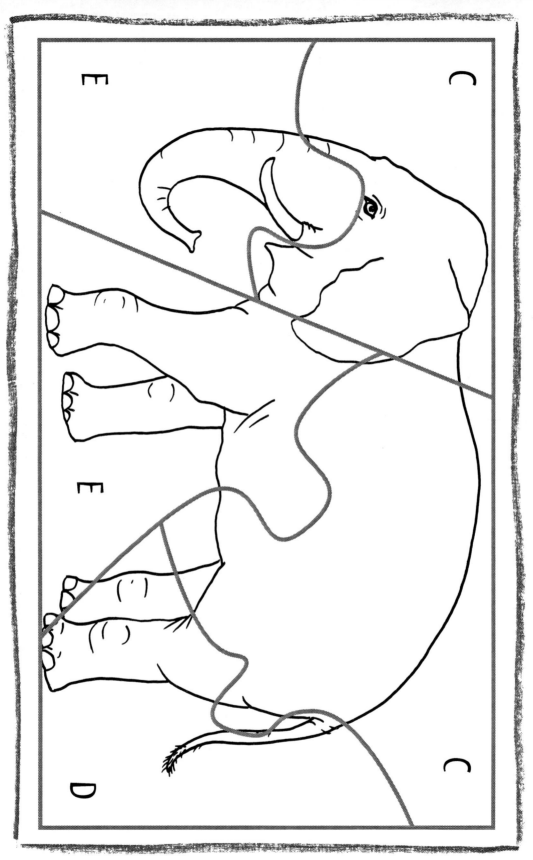

Sentence Completion Cards

Co-operation is needed because…

Being disrespectful is…

One way I co-operate with teachers is…

One way I co-operate with friends is…

One way I co-operate with family is…

When I need help, I wish others would…

I could help others by…

Working in a group is good because…

Inconsideration of others is…

Session 5: Anger Management

Aims

- to highlight what situations, people or places make pupils angry
- to highlight how pupils react physiologically when they are angry
- to highlight how pupils release their anger
- to examine the consequences of anger on others and ourselves
- to examine alternative strategies for dealing with anger
- to encourage pupils to apply what they learn to everyday life.

Resources

- Anger Prompt Card
- flip chart paper
- marker pens
- blue tack.

Welcome back and positive start

Welcome back pupils. Going around the circle each pupil is to complete the following round:

"Something I am pleased with about this week is…"

Introduction

Introduce the theme of anger, highlighting that the aims of the session are to examine pupil's natural reactions to anger, the consequences anger can have on others and us and to look at alternative strategies for dealing with anger.

Open discussion

Word association

Going around the circle each pupil is to think of another word that means angry. For example, mad, livid, furious, upset, enraged, vexed, annoyed, etc. Ask the questions:

- "What is anger?"
- "Who has ever felt angry?"

It may be necessary to distinguish between conflict (as an action) and anger (as a feeling).

My anger

Using the prompt card, invite pupils in turn to talk about their anger. The prompt can be placed in the centre of the circle for all pupils to see or passed around pupils so that they can read from it when it is their turn to talk.

- ▸ What situations make you feel angry?
  Being put down, shouted at, left out, treated unfairly, etc.

- ▸ How do you feel when you become angry?
  Fed-up, annoyed, hurt, like lashing out etc.

- ▸ How does your body react when you are angry?
  Goes red, heart beats faster, sweat, tense up, etc.

- ▸ What do you look like when you are angry?
  Face is scrunched up, hands go into fists, etc.

- ▸ What do you do when you are angry?
  Argue, lash out, fight, walk away, cry, etc.

- ▸ How do other people react to you when you're angry?
  Leave me alone, get involved, argue back, etc.

- ▸ What, if any, are the consequences of your anger outburst?
  Detention, isolation, grounding, losing friends, etc.

Anger management

Create a discussion regarding the different strategies pupils use to control their anger, calm themselves down or avoid getting angry.

Introduce other strategies and techniques and gain pupils opinions on using them, their effectiveness and their suitability.

- ▸ Deep breathing – in through the nose for a count of four and out through the mouth for a count of six.

- ▸ Visualisation – think of a relaxing image or a favourite place, draw it and imagine the experience.

- ▸ Think positively – I am in control of myself, I can control how I let my anger out, I am clever and I can handle this, it's okay to feel angry, I am happy with myself, I am in charge of my feelings. Remind yourself that the world is not out to get you – you are just experiencing some of the rough spots of daily life.

- ▸ Self-talk – slowly repeat a calm word or phrase to yourself, such as, take it easy, relax, chill-out, no big deal, keep calm, etc.

- ▸ Relaxation – do gentle exercises, listen to calming music, count to ten, count backwards, lie down and close your eyes, put your hands in your pockets.

- ▸ Use humour – instead of calling someone a name, stop and think what that name would look like; it may take the edge of your anger.

- ▶ Change your environment – if appropriate – walk away, ask for time out to calm down, have a special place to go, have a special person to talk to, ask for a 'cooling off' period and if you can talk later.

- ▶ Channel anger – punch a pillow, scream or yell on your own, stamp your feet on a solid floor, scribble hard, tear up unwanted newspapers or magazines, stamp on a cardboard box, do some sport or exercise.

- ▶ Imagination – imagine you are protected by a turtle shell and that the situation cannot hurt you, hide behind an imaginary shield, imagine cooling your thoughts by placing them in a freezer, imagine digging a hole for your angry thoughts and burying them, write down your angry thoughts and feelings and dispose of them imagining that they have gone away and that they are no longer with you.

- ▶ Cool down – drink water, take off unnecessary clothing, get some fresh air, wash your face in cold water.

Calming or alarming

Once anger has emerged there are things we do that escalate or defuse a situation. Split the group into two. Get one group to free-think things that we do that make a situation worse when we are angry, for example, blame, shout, hit, sulk. Get the other group to free-think things that make a situation better when we are angry, for example, understand, talk, involve a mediator, apologise.

To split the group use a characteristic of the pupils, for example, ask people with light hair to work in one group and pupils with dark hair to work in the other.

Reconvene the groups and discuss, looking at the consequences of our angry reactions.

Round

Going around the circle invite each pupil in turn to complete the following sentence:

"Next time I'm angry, I'm going to try…"

Conclude session

End the session on a positive note. Thank pupils for their willingness to try new ideas, honesty, hard work etc.

Anger Prompt Card

What situations make you feel angry?

Being put down, shouted at, left out, treated unfairly, etc.

How do you feel when you become angry?

Fed-up, annoyed, hurt, like lashing out, etc.

How does your body react when you are angry?

Goes red, heart beats faster, sweats, tenses up, etc.

What do you look like when you are angry?

Face is scrunched up, hands go into fists, etc.

What do you do when you are angry?

Argue, lash out, fight, walk away, cry, etc.

How do other people react to you when you're angry?

Leave me alone, get involved, argue back, etc.

What, if any, are the consequences of your anger outbursts?

Detention, isolation, grounding, lose friends, etc.

Session 6: Bullying

Aims

- to define bullying behaviour
- to highlight commonly held myths about bullying
- to discuss personal experiences of bullying
- to examine reasons behind bullying behaviour
- to highlight the effects of bullying on those on the receiving end
- to examine ways to prevent bullying in school
- to encourage pupils to apply what they learn to everyday life.

Resources

- flip chart paper
- marker pens
- blue tack
- Who Gets Bullied? worksheet – one per pupil.

Welcome back and positive start

Welcome back pupils. Going around the circle, each pupil is to complete the following round:

"Something nice I've done or said to another person this week is…"

Introduction

Introduce the theme of bullying, highlighting the aims of the session.

Myths and facts about bullying

Create an imaginary spectrum where one side of the line is true and the other is false. Read the following list of statements to the pupils getting them to move to one or the other end of the spectrum depending on whether they view the statement as true or false. If pupils don't know or believe it is sometimes true or sometimes false, they can stand in the middle of the spectrum.

Fact	Myth
▸ Anyone can be a bully.	▸ Bullying is just teasing.
▸ Bullying occurs roughly once every seven minutes.	▸ Some people deserve to be bullied.
▸ Some bullies are being bullied themselves.	▸ Only boys are bullies.
▸ Repeatedly calling someone names is bullying.	▸ It's snitching to tell an adult when you are being bullied.
▸ Some bullies have low esteem – that is why they pick on others.	▸ Bullying is a normal part of growing up.
▸ We can all make a difference in stopping bullying.	▸ The best way to deal with a bully is by frightening them or trying to get even.
▸ To threaten or frighten someone is bullying.	▸ People who are bullied may hurt for a while, but they'll get over it.
▸ To isolate someone is bullying.	

Defining bullying

Split the class into two groups. Give them five minutes to come up with a definition of 'bullying'.

Examples are:

▸ Long-standing violence.

▸ Wilful and conscious desire to hurt, threaten or frighten someone else.

▸ Hurting people's feelings and making their lives a misery.

▸ Where someone picks on somebody else who isn't as strong as him or her. It can sometimes be called teasing.

There are different forms of bullying:

▸ Physical bullying is hitting, pushing, spitting, punching, etc.

▸ Verbal bullying is using abusive or threatening language, making abusive telephone calls, threatening text messages, name calling, spreading rumours, etc.

▸ Silent bullying is manipulating or ruining friendships, making mean faces or rude gestures, ignoring and isolating.

Personal experiences

Allow time for pupils to talk about their personal experiences of bullying.

Has anyone ever been bullied?

- ▸ What did it feel like?
- ▸ What did you do?

Who gets bullied?

Hand out the worksheet 'Who Gets Bullied?' Pupils are to individually pick out the five most likely people to be bullied.

Reconvene the group getting pupils to feedback their list. The point to be made is that anyone can be bullied for any reason. You may want to read the following poem to pupils to reiterate this point.

You get it for being Jewish

You get it for being Black

You get it for being Chicken

And you get it for fighting back

You get it for being big and fat

You get it for being small

Oh those who get it, get it

For any damn thing at all.

(Taken from *Back in the Playground Blues* By Adrian Mitchell from Allison & Busby (1985) *Kingfisher Book of Children's Poetry* in Tattun and Herbert (1990) *Bullying: a Positive Response*, Cardiff: CIHE)

Why people bully

People bully for a whole range of reasons. Get the pupils to think of some reasons why people may bully others. For example:

- ▸ jealousy
- ▸ they are a victim of bullying
- ▸ to gain power
- ▸ to gain popularity
- ▸ for money.

Victims of bullying

How do you think people who are victims of bullying feel?

They might feel angry, scared, terrified, lonely, suicidal, petrified, nervous, edgy, anxious, apprehensive, isolated, sick, worried.

Read through the poem written by a victim of bullying:

> Day and day, I put up with this pain
> Their fists bruise my body; their words drive me insane
> They tear me apart with their insults and threats
> I live with their words, I just can't forget.
>
> Each night I go home and hide how I feel
> Out of this life, I've got a raw deal
> Can't tell the teacher, my dad or my mom
> I can't tell my friend, they'll all think I'm dumb
>
> They won't miss me; I'm pathetic and weak
> A way to end this pain is what I seek.

(Anonymous victim of bullying, Thrybergh School – taken from *Taking Action on Bullying*)

Combating bullying

Going around the circle invite each pupil to complete the following sentence by making a suggestion on how to combat bullying, specifically within school.

  "I could help prevent bullying by... "

For example:

- ▸ telling a teacher if I see someone being bullied
- ▸ making friends with the person being bullied
- ▸ making anti-bullying posters
- ▸ offering advice to the victim and/or bully
- ▸ promoting a non-bullying atmosphere
- ▸ making sure I never bully someone, even if I think it's a joke.

Conclude session

End the session on a positive note. Thank pupils for their ideas, understanding, hard work, kindness, etc.

Who Gets Bullied?

Pick out the five people most likely to get bullied

- ☐ Someone who is very clever
- ☐ Someone who is not very good at reading and writing
- ☐ Someone who is always telling tales
- ☐ Someone who is good at PE
- ☐ Someone who is no good at PE
- ☐ Someone who cries easily
- ☐ Someone who can stand up for themselves
- ☐ Someone who is a loner and has few friends
- ☐ Someone who has lots of friends
- ☐ Someone who is bossy
- ☐ Someone who is shy
- ☐ Someone who thinks they know everything
- ☐ Someone who enjoys a laugh
- ☐ Someone who asks the teacher questions a lot
- ☐ Someone who doesn't like getting dirty
- ☐ Someone who flies into a temper easily
- ☐ Someone whose parents are very rich
- ☐ Someone who does not wear designer gear
- ☐ Someone who is bigheaded
- ☐ Someone who is attractive
- ☐ Someone who wears glasses
- ☐ Someone who wears a brace
- ☐ Someone who is tall
- ☐ Someone who is short
- ☐ Someone who is overweight
- ☐ Someone who is thin
- ☐ Someone who is always helpful

Session 7: Review, Feedback and Evaluation

Aims

- to gain feedback on what pupils have gained from Circle Time
- to examine what skills pupils have developed or learnt and how they have or will apply them to their lives
- to clarify any areas
- to evaluate the content
- to present pupils with certificates of completion and celebrate successes.

Resources

- flip chart paper
- marker pens
- blue tack
- certificates – one per pupil
- Evaluation forms - one per pupil.

Welcome back and positive start

Welcome back pupils. Going around the circle each pupil is to complete the following round:

"Something good I have done this week is…"

Introduction

Explain to pupils that this last session is to gain feedback about what each individual believes they have learnt from undertaking the programme, how things may have changed as a result of what they have learnt and how they may apply any newly developed skills to their lives. In addition the session will allow for the opportunity to evaluate the programme content.

Programme content and feedback

Free-think the different topics involved in the programme.

Session 1: Setting the scene

Session 2: Listening

Session 3: Friends and friendship

Session 4: Respect, consideration and co-operation

Session 5: Anger management

Session 6: Bullying.

Record these on to a separate piece of large paper. Place two pieces of flip chart paper at either end of the room. Title one, positive feedback and the other negative feedback.

Allow pupils to write comments on each of the pieces of paper. They can talk to one another regarding their thoughts on the negative and positive aspects of the course.

Comments can include:

▶ parts of the programme they have enjoyed
▶ parts of the programme they have disliked
▶ parts of the programme they remember
▶ skills the topic taught.

Reconvene the group and discuss the comments in more depth.

Sentence completion rounds

Going around the circle, invite each pupil in turn to complete the following series of statements:

▶ "One thing I have learnt from this course is…"
▶ "The importance of learning this is…"
▶ "I have put this into practice by…"

Evaluation

Provide each pupil with an evaluation form to complete individually. Allow five minutes before reconvening the group. Ask each pupil to feedback verbally to the rest of the group two points from their evaluation form. Collect in evaluation forms after this exercise.

Certificate presentation

When handing out the certificates congratulate each pupil in turn for something you believe they have achieved or done well, for example, full   - attendance, co-operation, mature ideas, etc. Personalise each persons 'well done' statement.

Open discussion

Allow time for:

▶ clarification of any topics that pupils may require
▶ further feedback pupils require
▶ any questions
▶ provision of additional information or advice.

Games time

If time allows pupils can choose a game to play from the ones that have taken place in the programme or others that they know.

- Dumbstruck sports (Session 1)
- Magic keys (Session 2)
- Story time (Session 2)
- Friendship game (Session 3)
- Tangled (Session 4)
- Jigsaws (Session 5)

Conclude session

End the session on a positive note. Thank pupils for their participation, hard work, good ideas, skills, etc. throughout the course of the programme.

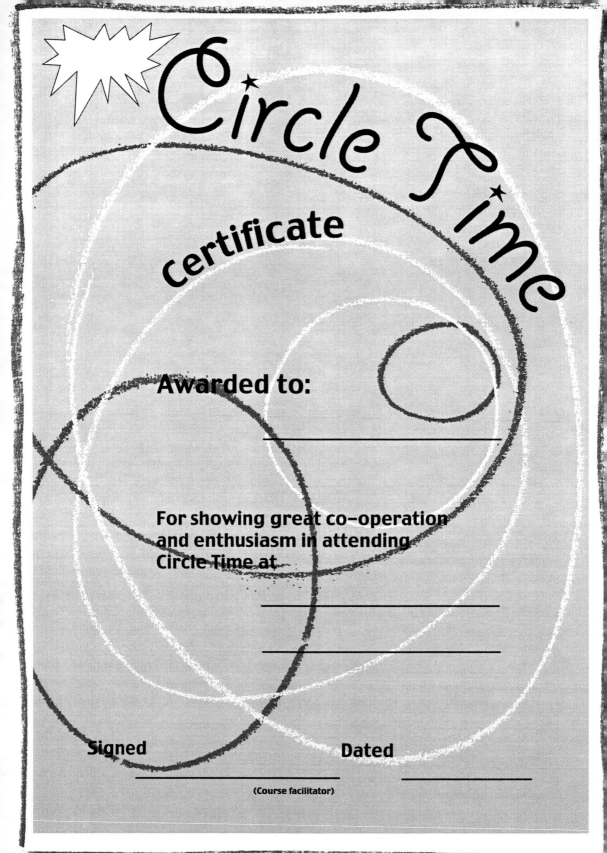

Circle Time

Certificate

Awarded to:

_____

For showing great co-operation
and enthusiasm in attending
Circle Time at

_____

_____

Signed

_____
(Course facilitator)

Dated

_____

Evaluation Form

Date

I have found this course:	I have enjoyed this course:
☐ Extremely useful	☐ A great deal
☐ Very useful	☐ A lot
☐ Of some use	☐ To some extent
☐ Of little use	☐ Not that much
☐ Of no use at all	☐ Not at all

Would you recommend this course to others?   ☐ YES   ☐ NO

Tick the words you feel apply to this course

☐ Interesting	☐ Easy	☐ Stimulating	☐ Difficult
☐ Topical	☐ Irrelevant	☐ Boring	☐ Thought provoking
☐ Fun	☐ Entertaining	☐ Disappointing	☐ Motivating
☐ Helpful	☐ Depressing	☐ Confusing	☐ Relaxing

Rate the following out of five
5 = very useful and 0 = not at all useful

☐ Worksheets	☐ Discussion
☐ Role-play	☐ Working in pairs
☐ Teacher talking	☐ Free-thinking ideas
☐ Setting rules	☐ Rounds

What I enjoyed most was…
_____
_____

What I enjoyed least was…
_____
_____

My suggestions for improving the course are:
_____
_____

Bibliography

Ashton, M & Varga, L. (1993) *101 Games for Groups*, Texas, Pro-ed,

Ballard, J. (1982) *Circle Book*, New York, Irvington.

Barnard, M. E. & Cartwright, C. (1996) *Programme Achieve*, East Sussex, ASG.

Benson, P.L., Galbraith, J. & Espeland, P. (1998) *What Teens Need to Succeed*, Minneapolis, Free Spirit.

Bliss, T., Robinson, G & Maines, B. (1995) *Developing Circle-Time*, Bristol, Lucky Duck Publishing Ltd.

Bliss, T. & Tetley, J. (1993) *Circle-Time a Resource Book for Infant, Junior and Secondary Schools*, Bristol, Lucky Duck Publishing Ltd.

Bond, T. (1986) *Games for Social and Life Skills*, Cheltenham, Stanley Thornes.

Britton, F. (2000) *Discovering Citizenship Through Active Learning in The Community*, Essex, CSV Education for Citizenship.

Brown, J. & Fabry, L. (1999) *Overcoming Bullying*, Milton Keynes, Chalkface Project.

Burt, S., Davis, G., Lister, J., Morgan, R. & O'Shea, S. (1999) *Six Years of Circle-Time*, Bristol: Lucky Duck Publishing Ltd.

Campaign for Real Education (2002) *What is Personal, Social and Health Education?*, York, CRE.

Collins (1979) *English Dictionary 21st Century Edition*, Aylesbury, Harper Collins.

Collins, M. (2001) *Circle Time for the Very Young*, Bristol, Lucky Duck Publishing Ltd.

Coppersmith, S. (1967) *The Antecedents of Self-Esteem*, San Francisco, WH Freeman.

Curry, M. (2001) *Building a Peaceful School*, Staffordshire, NASEN.

Curry, M. & Bromfield, C. (1994) *Personal and Social Education for Primary Schools Through Circle-Time*, Staffordshire, NASEN.

Curry, M. & Bromfield, C. (1998) *Circle-Time In-Service Training Manual*, Staffordshire, NASEN.

Dearling, A. & Armstrong, H. (1994) *The New Youth Games Book*, Dorset, Russel House Publishing.

DfES (1994) *Circular 1/94*, DfES.

Douglas, T. (1983) *Group Work Practice*, Tavistock.

Duboust, S. & Knight, P. (1995) *Group Activities for Personal Development*, Oxon, Speechmark.

Eldridge, R.M. (1999) *Towards a Policy For Spiritual Development – A Discussion Paper*, NCC, now QCA.

Elton, Lord (1989) *Discipline in Schools*, Report of Committee of Enquiry Chaired by Lord Elton London, HMSO.

Fuchs, B. (2002) *Group Games: Social Skills*, Oxon, Speechmark.

Harvey, M. (1999) *Mind Matters: A Resource Bank on Relationships*, London, Youth Clubs UK.

Harvey, M. (2000) *Mind Matters: A Resource Bank on Actions*, London, Youth Clubs UK.

Harvey, M. (2000) *Mind Matters: A Resource Bank on Self-Esteem*, London, Youth Clubs UK.

Kelly, A. (1996) *Talkabout: A Social Communication Skills Package*, Oxon, Speechmark.

Korfkamp, T. (1998) *Raising Self-Esteem and Building Self-Confidence Through Group Work*, Wolverhampton, WISARD.

Korfkamp, T. (1999) *Circle-Time: A Resource Pack For Teachers and School Staff*, Wolverhampton, WISARD

Long, R. (1999) *Exercising Self-Control*, Wales, NASEN

Long, R. (1999) *Friendships*, Wales, NASEN.

McConnon, S. (1989) *Active Learning: A Personal Skills Course for Young People*, Surrey, Macmillan Education Ltd.

McConnon, S. (1989) *Self-Esteem: A Personal Skills Course for Young People*, Surrey, Macmillan Education Ltd.

McConnon, S. (1989) *The Nature of Friendship: A Personal Skills Course for Young People*, Surrey, Macmillan Education Ltd.

McConnon, S. (1989) *The Skills of Friendship: A Personal Skills Course for Young People*, Surrey, Macmillan Education Ltd.

McConnon, S. (1990) *Interpersonal Communication: A Personal Skills Course for Young People*, Surrey, Macmillan Education Ltd.

McConnon, S. (1992) *Feelings: A Personal Skills Course for Young People*, Surrey, Macmillan Education Ltd.

McConnon, S. (1992) *Groups: A Personal Skills Course for Young People*, Surrey, Macmillan Education Ltd.

McConnon, S. (1992) *Making Decisions: A Personal Skills Course for Young People* Surrey, Macmillan Education Ltd.

McConnon, S. (1996) *Conflict: A Personal Skills Course for Young People,* Surrey, Macmillan Education Ltd.

Mosley, J. (1993) *Turn Your School Around,* Cambs, LDA.

Mosley, J. & Tew, M. (1999) *Quality Circle-Time in the Secondary School: A Handbook of Good Practice,* London, David Fulton.

Myers, J. (1998) *Inside the Circle Special,* Spring Edition.

Newton, C. & Wilson, D. (1995) *Circles of Friends,* Paper presented at EPS Nottingham.

Newton, C. & Wilson, D. (1999) *Circles of Friends,* Dunstable, Folens Ltd.

Perry, M. & Britton, S. (1996) *How To Do Drugs: Ideas For Drug Prevention,* London, Hope UK.

Peterson, J.S. (1993) *Talk With Teens About Self and Stress,* Minneapolis, Free Spirit.

Peterson, J.S. (1993) *Talk With Teen About Feelings, Family, Relationships and the Future,* Minneapolis, Free Spirit.

Portmann, R. (2002) *Group Games: Emotional Strength and Self-Esteem,* Oxon, Speechmark.

Pru Youth Action. *Taking Action on Bullying,* Wiltshire, Crime Concern Trust.

Qualifications and Curriculum Authority (1993) *Spiritual and Moral Development* – A Discussion Paper.

Rae, T. (2000) *Confidence, Assertiveness and Self-Esteem,* Bristol, Lucky Duck Publishing Ltd.

Robinson, G. & Maines, B. (1998) *Circle-Time Resources,* Bristol, Lucky Duck Publishing Ltd.

Schmuck & Schmuck (1987) In Korfkamp, T. (1998) *Raising Self-Esteem and Building Self-Confidence Through Group Work,* Wolverhampton, WISARD.

Settle, D. & Wise, C. (1986) *Choices, Materials and methods for Personal and Social Education,* Oxford, Basil Blackwell.

Tattum, D. & Herbert, G. (1990) *Bullying: A Positive Response: Advice For parents, Governors and Staff in School,* Cardiff, CIHE.

White, M. (1999) *Magic Circles: Building self-Esteem Through Circle-Time,* Bristol, Lucky Duck Publishing.

Wolverhampton Anti-Bullying Project. *A Guide For The Victims and Their Families of Bullying,* Wolverhampton, WCSP & WRP.

www.bullying.co.uk
www.circletime.com
www.dfes.gov.uk
www.luckyduck.co.uk